Putting on Christ
by Thomas Hooker
with chapters by C. Matthew McMahon

Copyright Information

Putting on Christ by Thomas Hooker, with chapters by C. Matthew McMahon
Edited by Therese B. McMahon

Copyright ©2024 by Puritan Publications and A Puritan's Mind®

Some language and grammar has been updated from any original manuscripts. Any change in wording or punctuation has not changed the intent or meaning of the original author(s) and has been made to aid the modern reader.

Published by Puritan Publications
A Ministry of A Puritan's Mind® in Crossville, TN.
www.apuritansmind.com
www.puritanpublications.com
www.gracechepeltn.com

All rights reserved. No part of this publication may be reproduced, stored in a retrieval system or transmitted in any form by any means, electronic, mechanical, photocopy, recording or otherwise, without the prior permission of the publisher, except as provided by USA copyright law.

This Print Edition, 2024
Electronic Edition, 2024

Manufactured in the United States of America

ISBN: 978-1-62663-491-6
eISBN: 978-1-62663-490-9

Table of Contents

The Importance of Vivification 5
First Meeting House in Connecticut 19
Rev. Thomas Hooker's House 20
Part 1: The Soul's Ingrafting into Christ 21
    Two Aspects of Implantation 22
    Christ Entering a Soul 25
    God's Immediate Presence 27
    The Arrival of Christ to a Humble Soul 29
    Failing to Recognize the Work of Christ 33
    Uses of Implantation 36
Part 2: The Soul's Possession of Christ 43
    The Humility Needed 47
    Putting on Christ in Three Ways 48
    Three Means to Put on Christ 51
    The Second Means of Putting on Christ 54
    Faith in Motion 55
    Meditation a Grand Help 58
    Dwelling in God 61
    No Advantage to Satan or the Flesh 62
    Making Provision for the Flesh 63
    Point of Instruction 66
    Making Provision Yields Obedience to Sin 68
    Adding Strength to Corruptions 71
    Hindering Grace 73

Getting a Right Heart 77
Appendix: Spiritual Munition 87
Other Works from Puritan Publications Concerning *Coming to Christ* 97

The Importance of Vivification
by C. Matthew McMahon, Ph.D., Th.D.

"...have put on the new man, which is renewed in knowledge after the image of him that created him," (Col. 3:10).

You may be aware of what it means to "mortify sin," that is, *to put it to death*. How do you do that? Hold that thought. To continue, as a Christian, as a "new man", you have been made *new* by the Spirit, but you still have a stinking, rotting corpse in you called the "old man," with that putrid corruption you wish you could get rid of. He's dead, but that dead corpse rots away and attempts to revive old habits in you. Daily, you have to kill sin. But, there is more to killing sin than just putting it to death. The "space" taken up by sin being killed in mortification must be replaced or filled with *life*, and new habits. This is *walking* in the Spirit. This is *putting on* Christ. Living in the power of the Spirit is about believing and acting to reverse the fall in your daily walk. Yes, the Spirit has reversed the fall in you by regeneration. He takes the works of Christ and applies that work to your soul, gives you a new heart and a new mind, and you respond to the Gospel by faith, and take Christ as King. However, that does not mean the struggle with sin instantly ends. Yes, you still have that old, dead, stinking, rotting corpse to deal with.

Sin quenches the power of the Spirit in

Christians; sin is a retreating *back* to the fall. You've been changed, you are a new man or woman in Christ, but you retreat back to the stinking corpse to try and revive it at various points in your daily walk.

As Christians, we should be thoroughly aware that we must fight against breaking the commandments of God and we ought to be at war with bringing reproach on Christ when we sin. We transgress the Law of God, as James comprehensively says, "For whosoever shall keep the whole law, and yet offend in one point, he is guilty of all," (James 2:10). All sin is diametrically opposed to the entirety of God's revealed will. To sin is *not living* (not walking) in the power of the Spirit, but rejecting that power; that grieves the Spirit. We choose to sin rather than put on Christ. But this is part of the point. Old habits must be killed, and new habits must be put in their place. Mortification must occur, but also vivification *must also* occur.

Scripture repeatedly directs us to mortify (or kill) the deeds of the flesh, and to not quench the Spirit; which is squelching sanctification, a *squelching of vivification*. Romans 6:12 says, "Let not sin therefore reign in your mortal body, that ye should obey it in the lusts thereof." We should not allow carnal delights to rule us, but rather, we ought to kill all of them by the power of the Spirit. Romans 13:14, "But put ye on the Lord Jesus Christ, and make not provision for the flesh, to fulfill the lusts thereof." No provision, or *instance*, should be given to reviving the fall in us. Instead, we out to kill sin, and replace those old habits by putting on Christ.

As a result, we are always on guard as warriors fighting vehemently for our lives. Galatians 5:24, "And they that are Christ's have crucified the flesh with the affections and lusts." This is a graphic depiction of death since it is reminiscent of Christ's death. Paul is not only saying that sin should be *killed*, but that it should bring to mind the death of Christ and His sacrifice *for that sin*. We ought to live "as obedient children, not fashioning yourselves according to the former lusts in your ignorance," (1 Peter 1:14). We not only kill sin through godly means, but using the God-given godly sense we have, we should run far away from its grasp and allurement, "Dearly beloved, I beseech you as strangers and pilgrims, abstain from fleshly lusts, which war against the soul; Having your conversation honest among the Gentiles: that, whereas they speak against you as evildoers, they may by your good works, which they shall behold, glorify God in the day of visitation," (1 Peter 2:11-12). If we do not take this mortification of sin seriously, and kill our sin, *then our sin will kill us*, "For if ye live after the flesh, ye shall die: but if ye through the Spirit do mortify the deeds of the body, ye shall live," (Romans 8:13). Colossians 3:5 says, "Mortify therefore your members which are upon the earth; fornication, uncleanness, inordinate affection, evil concupiscence, and covetousness, which is idolatry." Kill or be killed is the warfare of the Christian. Who will win – lust or the Christian? What habits will they exercise themselves in?

Will they allow the old man to try and revive their old ways, or will they concur with the work of the Spirit and put on Christ? You might be saying, "I don't know what it means to *put on Christ?*"

The spiritual war we face is linked with the physical war; for example, we should do everything we can in order to abstain from sin (*mortifying it*). That may even entail knowing the reasons why God gave us such things as "eyes." Our eyes were not meant to be fascinated with things pertaining to lust. Joseph, for example, was successful in putting off Potiphar's wife, but he went to prison for it. The temptation of sin is a great burden to the righteous soul. It would be nice if when we were temped to sin, that if we overcome it, it would be vanquished in that act one time. It would be especially wonderful for those who struggle with specific sins that have *yet* to be mortified, that once they *put them off*, those sins would never tempt them again. But this is not the way God has so ordered the Christian walk. Temptation to sin comes again and again. If one is only looking to kill sin, without adding in new habits of holiness (vivification), what will be the result? One will say that before being converted they swore terribly, and now they do not; but another Christian who swore terribly, still deals with that in their mind and must be in constant awareness of it. Sin is comprised of so many parts that until heaven, the believer must be under the burden of fighting against temptation to sin, and not simply just particular sins, but all of sin.

Consider that sinning before God is so terrible, that God directs the Christians to think of fighting temptation with full armor, considering Ephesians 6 and the full armor of God that is given to them. It is God's armor that the Christian must wear. It is Christ, "*put on* Christ." And it is a very special armor at that which has nothing to protect the back so that *retreating* is impossible. They must always engage themselves in the battle. With this armor, with holy habits formed in them, they are able, in looking to Christ, to evade the temptations of the world the flesh and the devil. Will they always do this? When we are in heaven, filled up and changed with heavenly delicacies, when we are satisfied with Christ and all he gives us, why would we be captivated with the trash of sinners and the waywardness of this world (*cf.* Luke 15:16)? It will be impossible when we are there in glory. But here, on earth, if we are occupied with the most serious matters of heaven, what would call us back to earthly, vain, and childish things? Do we not grow, change and *put on* better things? Such a holy mindset which grows in this way casts a great blow against all wicked temptations.

Add to the godly armor of the Christian the supernatural work of godly fear, and the recipe for vivification grows further. Godly fear is a grace from the Holy Spirit which is essential to dealing with both temptation and sin, as well as helping you as a Christian "*put on* Christ." The pardoned soul knows to seek the growth of grace. It is the soul's delight to seek the growth of grace from Jesus Christ. "... grace and truth came by Jesus Christ," (John 1:17). Such grace enables the soul to serve Christ in a way that *God accepts*. Here is the rub on this – what *God accepts* is only what *he prescribes*, and this is *only* through Jesus Christ, by the power of the Spirit of Christ. Anything else is not acceptable no matter how much one might be sincere in what they do. A person may hide themselves in a locked room so as not to participate in the world, they retreat, but this is hiding, not mortification, and not putting on Christ. Employ anything else, (bite your upper lip and try to push through temptations in your own strength), and one is employing the use of human means, not godly, Spirit-filled means, to try and overcome sin. When people try to avoid sin, or just push themselves to overcome it by their own strength without using God's ordained means, not only will they not mortify sin, but they will not create the godly habits they need to *put on Christ*. "Wherefore we receiving a kingdom which cannot be moved, let us have grace, whereby we may serve God acceptably with reverence and godly fear," (Heb. 12:28). Serving God is done in humble reverence or modesty, coupled with a fearful caution. It is an exercise in the principle of godly fear.

    The grace of Christ is the cause of all benefits that the pardoned soul receives. This grace, this unmerited favor through the merits of Christ, is the cause of every success in the soul.[2] It is applied by the Spirit, and motivates the soul to serve God in a pleasing manner. In bringing Christ to every duty, the pardoned soul finds favor with God, and so, all his works performed in accordance with the directives of God, are received as if they are done by Christ himself, which is a "putting on of Christ." Christ is the greatest gift of grace that the pardoned soul can receive because he colors all the duties and all the works the soul performs under his blood. The Spirit applies this gracious gift of Christ, to the pardoned soul who clothes himself with Christ each day; that soul *puts on Christ*. Again, you are directed to this end, "But put ye on the Lord Jesus Christ, and make not provision for the flesh, to fulfil the lusts thereof," (Rom. 13:14). In this way, all acceptable service to God is accomplished, as a result of Christ's merit applied through the Spirit in the duties that God prescribes. God never, ever, accepts duties that he has not prescribed. Christians must be very careful to bring what God desires.

However, laying aside that which is filthy is not so easily done, and putting in its place that which is holy is even more difficult in many ways. Ephesians speaks of laying aside lying sin (4:25). Colossians speaks of laying aside evil practices (3:9). Hebrews speaks of laying aside

---

[2] "The operations of grace are ours, but the power that enables us is from God. Our preservation from evil, and perseverance in good, is a most free unmerited favor, the effect of his renewed grace in the course of our lives." Bates, William, *The Harmony of the Divine Attributes*, (London: J. Darby, 1674) 323.

weights that weigh down (12:1), *besetting sin* (original sin of all kinds). Take off the old man and put on the new man. Take off the old garments and put on new garments. Garments sprinkled by blood, covered in the blood of Christ. "*But put ye on* the Lord Jesus Christ, and make not provision for the flesh, to fulfil the lusts thereof," (Rom. 13:14). However, sin is not something that Christians can simply brush away, or simply lay aside like a cloak. How wonderful would it be to easily wash remaining sin off with a bar of soap? So, what are you to do? How are holy habits created? How is *putting on* Christ achieved? This is exactly what Thomas Hooker is going to show you in this work.

First, Hooker will show you what it means to be engrafted into Jesus Christ. Then he will show you what it means to have your soul possess Christ day by day; to put on Christ. The engraftment of the soul in Christ is a key concept that lies at the heart of Christian theology, embodying the relationship between the believer and Christ. At the core of Hooker's beginning discussion is the acknowledgment of the Lord Jesus Christ's sovereign claim over the humbled soul, the born again believer who is arrested by Christ and renewed to understand the importance of the Gospel. "Now when I passed by thee, and looked upon thee, behold, thy time was the time of love; and I spread my skirt over thee, and covered thy nakedness: yea, I sware unto thee, and entered into a covenant with thee, saith the Lord GOD, and thou becamest mine," (Ezek. 16:8). The imagery of engraftment serves as a powerful metaphor for the integration of the believer's soul with Christ's mystical body, marking a transition from a state of separation (children of wrath) to one of intimate union (adopted as sons and daughters of the most High God). This is contingent upon the soul's submission and humility in being renewed by the Spirit, creating the conditions necessary for Christ's divine possession of the soul.

Hooker explains the dynamics of Christ's holy possession in the initial step in the process involving the soul's recognition of its own wickedness and incapacity to elude the inherent consequences of original, and actual, sin. It is within this context of regeneration, and their acknowledged need and desperation that Christ intervenes, offering protection and pledging as Surety to assume responsibility for the soul's complete redemption. This role of Christ is reminiscent of the cities of refuge in Numbers 35, where individuals pursued for manslaughter could find asylum. Analogously, the soul pursued by the consequences of sin finds refuge in Christ, who delivers it from the avenger's reach.

Christ's work and merit undertaken on behalf of the soul encompasses three critical areas of deliverance: satisfying divine justice, overcoming Satanic temptation, and subduing the power of sin. These assurances address the anxieties that the believer, the repentant soul, has in lieu of being transferred from the dominion of darkness into the kingdom of God's beloved

Son, offering a complete salvation that extends beyond mere pardon. This includes liberation from sin's dominion and the adversarial schemes of Satan. It allows believers who are sincerely converted, to mortify sin, and put on Christ.

Hooker shows that the sovereignty of Christ's claim over the soul manifests in two distinct yet interconnected actions: the undertaking for the soul's protection and the disposition of the soul for His sovereign purposes. The metaphor of being engrafted implies not only a protective enclosure but also a nurturing intention, by which the soul is cultivated for its highest good to the glory of God.

Christ's protective role is further seen through the legal metaphor of *bailment*, where Christ stands as the guarantor for the soul, acquitting it from the claims of divine justice and the Father's wrath against sin. This act of mediation is *pivotal*, assuring the believer of Christ's efficacy in securing their freedom from condemnation and giving them eternal life, not merely a temporary fix.

Moreover, the confrontation with sin and temptation reveals Christ's authoritative dominion, in which He exercises His power to repel the forces of darkness and assert His rightful claim over the soul as one of *his seed*. This dynamic of conquest and liberation is vividly portrayed through the imagery of leading captivity captive, underscoring Christ's victory over sin and death.

What is the engrafted soul's response? The transformation seen in the engraftment of the soul in Christ's mystical body necessitates a responsive engagement from the believer. Yes, that means you have to *do* something. This response is characterized by a dual aspect: 1) passive reception, and 2) active calling. The soul, emptied of self-sufficiency and pride, becomes a receptive vessel for the continued work of divine grace and mercy, since it has been born from above, and made a new creature. This openness and readiness in sanctification is crucial for the instilling of the virtues and gifts that flow from union with Christ day to day to empower believers to walk in the Spirit.

The *active calling* of the soul, motioned by the indwelling power of the Holy Spirit, shows the believer's cooperative participation in the divine life – the life of God in the soul of man. It is where the Christian soul responds to God's call both as a reflection and an affirmation of the divine initiative. The exchange between God and the soul, marked by mutual recognition and commitment, culminates in the exercise of faith, which is both a gift and a task entrusted to the believer.

Once the soul is "in the Beloved" there is a radical reorientation of the believer's identity and purpose, grounded in the sovereign claim of King Jesus and culminating in a dynamic union characterized by protection, reformation, and active participation in the work of the Kingdom. Through this spiritual union, the believer is equipped to navigate the complexities of existence with resilience and hope, anchored in the assurance of Christ's resolute love and power.

After a soul is engrafted, Hooker explains that the soul *takes possession of Christ* to its fullest. Central to Hooker's point is the concept of "putting on" Christ, a process that involves both faith for justification (engrafting) and sanctification (the mortification of sin, and the new habits that are put on in the walk of a new life). Hooker emphasizes that even those who have received Christ and experienced the dawn of salvation in their hearts must *continually* seek comfort and grace from Christ for every spiritual service required by God.

Hooker explains the *process* of sanctification as a *daily necessity* for believers, urging them to glean strength and quickening from Christ for the fulfillment of divine duties and overcoming personal corruptions. He illustrates this necessity through the analogy of clothing, suggesting that just as one puts on garments, so must Christians put on Christ to be fitted and ready for any divine mission or directive. This metaphor extends to the idea that Christ measures and applies grace to each believer's infirmities, offering suitable and timely help for every condition, in any religious service.

Hooker shows that the various dangers and impediments to spiritual growth, such as pride, lust, and malice, can squelch growth in sanctification and hinder both killing sin, and putting on Christ. He shows that believers have a great need to constantly seek Christ's strength to overcome sin. In this, he shows that the issue of making *no provision* for the flesh to fulfill its lusts, as stated in Romans 13:14, is part of the vivification process. Mortifying sin is connected to the sanctifying work of the Spirit in putting on Christ at every opportunity. He warns against the dangers of allowing sin and corruption to take hold when the Spirit provides them with opportunities to flourish. He explains the need for a life of humility, submission, and obedience to God and his word, in which grace and divine assistance are sought daily from the Lord Jesus, and the virtue of the word is pulled from Scripture, and followed *step by step*.

The volume concludes with an annexed sermon preached at the funeral of Mr. Wilmott, a minister of Clare in Suffolk, which serves to underscore the importance of godly ministers as spiritual fathers and defenders of the faith. Hooker commends faithful ministers for their role in leading their congregations in prayer, repentance, and obedience to God's Word, while also mourning the loss of such spiritual leaders as a great loss to the church and society.

Overall, *Putting on Christ* is a rich theological treatise that encourages believers to live a life deeply connected to Christ. It is not merely killing sin, but continually seeking His grace and strength to fulfill God's will and overcome personal sin by creating new habits formed (vivification) while old habits are destroyed (mortification). This work serves as a reminder of the ongoing need for sanctification and the fundamental role of supernatural faith and obedience in the Christian life.

In Christ's grace and mercy,
C. Matthew McMahon, Ph.D., Th.D.
From My study, February, 2024
"...search the Scriptures..." (John 5:39).
www.apuritansmind.com
www.puritanpublications.com
www.gracechapeltn.com
www.reformedsynod.com

First Meeting House in Connecticut

The picture is believed to be a correct representation of the first house ever erected in Connecticut for Christian worship, built in 1635. Some of the lumber of the first house is still in existence, a portion of it being used in the construction of the *Centre Congregational Church*.

Rev. Thomas Hooker's House

The above Is a front view of the house of Rev. Thomas Hooker, first minister of the gospel in Connecticut. The projection in front (the A under the window) was called the *porch* and was used as his study. The building stood on the north side of School street, and the drawing was made immediately before it was taken down.

Part 1:
The Soul's Ingrafting into Christ[1]

Malachi 3:1, "Behold, I will send my messenger, and he shall prepare the way before me: and the Lord, whom ye seek, shall suddenly come to his temple, even the messenger of the covenant, whom ye delight in: behold, he shall come, saith the LORD of hosts."

  As we begin, we need to consider what we desire to accomplish and aim to do. Our goal is to demonstrate the way Christ's merits are applied to the soul, leading to possession of grace in this life and happiness in the next. For a soul to partake of this saving grace, two critical processes must occur: preparation and implantation. Since a sinner naturally lacks grace and is incapable of receiving it, preparation is essential. This preparation involves actions from both God and the sinner. God disrupts the harmful connection between sin and the soul, drawing us away from sin towards Himself. On our part, it involves harnessing our heart's regenerated condition through two actions: feeling genuine sorrow for our sins and humbling ourselves before God. These steps are necessary to overcome two major barriers to sincere faith: complacency, where the soul, blinded, feels no need for improvement and thus

---

[1] *The Soul's Ingrafting into Christ*. By Thomas Hooker, (1586-1647), (LONDON, Printed by J. H. for Andrew Crooke, at the sign of the Bear in Paul's Church-yard), 1637.

does not seek it, leading to a lack of desire for change due to a misunderstanding of sin's gravity; and the misguided *scramble* for personal comfort and superficial remedies, a trap that results in reliance on one's efforts rather than God's grace, mistaken for true salvation. Through this process, the soul learns to renounce all false securities and, acknowledging its *nothingness*, becomes ready for Christ to be its all.

Throughout this journey, the soul experiences a transition similar to the Israelites' journey from Egypt, through the wilderness, to Canaan, symbolizing moving from a state of natural sinfulness (Egypt), through the law (Moses) and repentance (wilderness), to embracing Christ (Joshua and Canaan). Like a graft that is cut, pared, and then engrafted into another stock, the soul is prepared through repentance and humility for implantation into Christ.

Two Aspects of Implantation

Our discussion on the work of being implanted into Christ will cover two aspects:
1. A general explanation.
2. An exploration of its components.

Implantation into Christ, generally, is the Spirit's work, enabling the humbled sinner to possess Christ and partake in His spiritual blessings. This involves the sinner being passively possessed by Christ, as highlighted in Galatians 4:9 and Philippians 3:12, emphasizing the soul's receptive rather than active role in this divine relationship. "My little children, of whom I travail in birth again until Christ be formed in you," (Gal. 4:19). "Not as though I had already attained, either were already perfect: but I follow after, if that I may apprehend that for which also I am apprehended of Christ Jesus," (Phil. 3:12).

In various aspects of Christian life—calling, justification, adoption, and sanctification—we see a pattern of being *possessed* by Christ and sharing in the spiritual riches He offers. These stages illustrate how Christ draws us closer, frees us from sin's guilt and power, adopts us as children with all associated privileges, and imprints His image upon us, marking us as His own.

This entire reformation is orchestrated by God's Spirit. Just as a branch cannot graft itself onto a vine, the Spirit that brings us to repentance is the same one that unites us with Christ, fulfilling the prophecy of John the Baptist as our guiding scripture from Malachi 3:1 reveals. This prophecy foretells the coming of a messenger to prepare the way for the Lord, promising the sudden arrival of the Lord to His temple, a messenger of the covenant in whom we delight, affirming, "Behold, he shall come, saith the Lord of Hosts."

In this passage, we are guided to observe two aspects related to John the Baptist. First, we examine the role of John the Baptist as God's messenger, whose duty was to prepare the way for Christ. Second, we consider the consequence of his work: the Lord will suddenly *come into* His temple. However, to fully understand the message, we must clarify two terms: "temple" and "Christ's coming into the temple."

The term "temple" has both a literal meaning and a mystical or spiritual interpretation. In this context, "temple" refers to the Church of God, which encompasses the community of faithful individuals who serve God with sincerity. More specifically, each believer who lives faithfully is considered a temple of God, as stated in 2 Corinthians 6:10, "Ye are the temple of the Holy Ghost." This comparison draws on the image of the material temple in Jerusalem, which was filled with the glory of the Lord and chosen as His dwelling place. Similarly, a humbled and prepared heart serves as the Lord's temple, where He takes residence, governs, and promises to provide for eternally. Just as a person resides in a house prepared for them, so does the Lord dwell in a humbled soul. In this way, we understand what is meant by "temple."

Regarding "the coming of the Lord into his temple," this term also demands a spiritual interpretation. The Lord's coming signifies His arrival to take possession of a soul that has been rightly prepared. It's important to note that the Lord Christ approaches as a King, preceded by a harbinger to prepare everything for Him. A King's arrival is characterized by two actions: taking sovereign possession of His domain and bringing

His own furnishings. Similarly, Christ takes full possession of the soul and mercifully provides for it.

Having explained these terms, the message becomes clear: when John the Baptist, through the power of the Word and the Spirit of contrition and humiliation, prepares the souls of God's servants, making them humbled and willing to submit to God's will, then the Lord Jesus will swiftly come. He will assert His command as a King, take possession of a humble soul, and generously provide for it. Christ requires nothing more than a prepared and emptied soul to which He brings ample provision of vocation, adoption, justification, and sanctification.

Christ Entering a Soul

From this explanation, we can draw two doctrinal points:

1. The Lord Jesus cannot be prevented from entering a humbled soul.

2. The Lord Christ assumes control of the soul as a King would, committing to care for it.

The first point to grasp is that Christ cannot be prevented from entering a soul that is *truly* humbled. He comes quickly, setting aside all other concerns as if they held no importance to Him, focused solely on entering a heart that has been prepared for Him. Christ does not approach the lost and wicked in their sin, nor does He heed the calls of the wealthy or save the prestigious;

instead, He eagerly seeks to dwell within a *humble* soul. It's as though, speaking with utmost respect, He leaves behind all company, abandoning even the heavens and the blessed angels, desiring only to reside within and cherish a heart that is humble and broken. This urgency is highlighted by the phrase "he comes suddenly," indicating His readiness to forsake all else for the sake of taking possession of a broken soul. The Scripture goes to great lengths to express God's weighty affection and the joy He finds in a humble soul, emphasizing His desire to not just visit but to live with, dwell within, and even rest within a heart that is contrite.

Luke 15:16 illustrates this through the parable of the prodigal son's *father*, who, upon seeing his son's decision to return and admit his sins, didn't wait for the son to make amends or reach him but instead ran to meet him, demonstrating compassion and love before the son could utter a single word. This narrative highlights four actions by the father: he saw his son from afar, felt compassion, ran to meet him, and kissed him, disregarding the son's past of recklessness and wastefulness, focusing solely on his *humble* return. This shows the immeasurable extent of God's willingness to welcome a humbled soul, further exemplified by the father's immediate actions to restore his son's dignity and status within the family, irrespective of his previous rebellion.

Similarly, Luke 15:4 compares this to a shepherd who leaves ninety-nine sheep to find the one that is lost, emphasizing God's dedication to reclaiming a lost soul, symbolizing His relentless pursuit and the joy of bringing a strayed soul back into His fold, regardless of its ability to return on its own. This parable demonstrates God's boundless generosity and eagerness to bring a humble sinner to everlasting happiness.

Matthew 13:45 uses the parable of the pearl to further illustrate God's kingdom, likening it to a merchant finding a priceless pearl and selling everything to possess it. This pearl represents God's mercy, grace, and salvation through Christ, with the merchant symbolizing every sinner in need of God's mercy. The act of selling everything to buy the pearl signifies a total renunciation of sin and self-reliance, embracing God's terms for salvation. This teaches that true value is found in God's mercy and grace, attainable by those willing to forsake all else for His sake.

God's Immediate Presence

The reasons for God's immediate presence in a humble soul are manifold:

1. Christ's mission, as mandated by God the Father, is to seek and save the lost (Matthew 15:24, Luke 19:10), emphasizing His dedication to finding those made aware of their own misery and incapacity to save themselves, ready to be guided and saved by Him.

2. This mission reflects God's determination to fulfill His purpose, ensuring that no soul aware of its

need for divine guidance and salvation will be overlooked or abandoned.

In this way, the essence of Christ's coming and His Father's sending Him is to secure salvation for the lost sinner, demonstrating a commitment to not only seek but to save those who are humbly awaiting His redemption.

Because a humble and broken soul is ideally suited to display the magnificence of God's grace and the salvation offered through Christ, such individuals are the most fitting recipients of God's reforming work. They provide the perfect backdrop for showcasing the splendor of God's redemptive efforts, as outlined in Ephesians 2:11-12, "Wherefore remember, that ye being in time past Gentiles in the flesh, who are called Uncircumcision by that which is called the Circumcision in the flesh made by hands; that at that time ye were without Christ, being aliens from the commonwealth of Israel, and strangers from the covenants of promise, having no hope, and without God in the world." And previously, "For by grace are ye saved through faith; and that not of yourselves: it is the gift of God: Not of works, lest any man should boast," (Eph. 2:8-9). These verses show that God orchestrates *everything* according to His will, aiming to glorify His grace. A humble soul, recognizing its own unworthiness and relying solely on God's grace and favor, exemplifies the ideal canvas to illustrate the overwhelming impact of salvation and God's grace. This soul acknowledges its undeservedness of mercy, making it a prime example of God's incredible work. This is where everything from start to finish is attributed to grace, echoing the sentiment of Zechariah during the temple's construction, where grace is celebrated as the foundation and completion of all things. "And I will pour upon the house of David, and upon the inhabitants of Jerusalem, the spirit of grace and of supplications" (Zech. 12:10).

In contrast, a proud heart resists God's grace, claiming some credit for itself and thereby obstructing the full appreciation of God's mercy in Christ. In this way, a humble soul serves as the best venue to observe the vastness of redemption and salvation, where one can truly say, "Look what the Lord has done," marveling at His work, "Consider the work of God," (Eccl. 7:13). Just as a wise individual chooses a residence that upholds his reputation and meets all his needs, so Christ finds His dwelling in a humble heart, the most suitable place to manifest His glory. The logic follows that if God has prepared a heart for His dwelling, refusing to complete this work would imply a lack of power or wisdom, attributes that cannot be ascribed to an omnipotent and omniscient God. Therefore, God, having prepared a soul for His glory, will *assuredly* bestow grace and salvation upon it.

The Arrival of Christ to a Humble Soul

Since all obstacles that could prevent Christ from entering such a soul are eliminated, His arrival becomes *inevitable*. Any potential hindrance would stem either from God or the soul itself. However, a truly broken heart (one regenerated) has already surrendered any self-love or adherence to sin, clearing the path for Christ's further work. The humbled soul desires Christ's rule, having discarded sin and self-governance. Revelation 3:20 depicts Christ as eagerly awaiting entry, knocking even on the doors of the most resistant hearts, offering redemption and salvation in place of corruption and sin. "Behold, I stand at the door, and knock: if any man hear my voice, and open the door, I will come in to him, and will sup with him, and he with me," (Rev. 3:20). Christ's promise to enter upon the door's opening leaves no doubt of His *readiness* to occupy a humbled heart, which has already been opened by the Spirit to His governance.

In this way, if Christ's rule and the glorification of His mercy are to be achieved without any impediment from either party, the prepared soul should anticipate Christ's immediate presence. This affirms the assurance of Christ's entry into a heart made ready through humility and repentance, which are gifts of the Spirit.

[Question:] I admit, I am willing to part with anything (and if I truly know myself) there is no sin that I am not ready to let go of. I have turned away from my sins and renounced myself, yet I find no comfort.

Therefore, either this teaching is incorrect, or my heart has not been healed.

[Answer:] Is this how you feel? Then it means Christ has come to you, but you have not *recognized* His presence. "And Jacob awaked out of his sleep, and he said, Surely the LORD is in this place; and I knew it not," (Gen. 28:16). When Jacob woke from his sleep, he realized, surely the Lord is in this place, and he did not know it. Similarly, the Lord is working on your soul, and yet you are unaware of Him.

[Question:] But is it possible for Christ to be present and not be noticed?

[Answer:] Yes, it happens quite often, and there are two types of obstacles:

1. Those from our side.
2. Those from Christ's side.

The obstacles from our side are fourfold:

1. Christ has entered your soul, but you do not recognize Him. In Matthew 14:26, when Christ was closest to offering comfort, they mistook Him for a spirit walking on the water who was meant to terrify them. Similarly, you might feel repulsed by your sins and think this isn't Christ's doing, *but it is*. Jesus Christ is there, and you do not see Him. In John 20:15-16, Mary Magdalene longed for Christ's presence, mistaking Him for the gardener, and asked about the Savior from the Savior Himself. She mistook him and did not recognize him. Likewise, a heartbroken sinner seeks a Savior; if you wish to know how to find favor with God, ask a poor

sinner. It is Christ who inspires you to seek Him, and you are seeking Christ with the help of Christ, like using a candle's light to search for the candle itself.

2. You may not notice our Savior when He arrives; He comes quietly and sometimes goes unnoticed. For instance, to His disciples locked in a room, He appeared suddenly among them (Luke 24). You might dwell on your sins, wondering how grace could reach such a heart. While focused on your corruption, you cannot see Christ. It wasn't Hagar's inability *to see* that prevented her from seeing the well; she simply wasn't looking for it. In this way, we may sit in despair, with Christ within us, yet fail to look for Him. A person waiting for a nobleman might retreat to a corner and weep if the nobleman doesn't arrive at the expected time, thinking he has caused offense, all the while the nobleman has arrived and been present for some time without his notice. Similarly, while we languish over our sins, thinking Christ has not come, we might fall into despair, and during this, Christ arrives without our notice.

3. A person in a dungeon cannot see the sunlight, no matter how brightly it shines outside; in the same way, when the Son of Righteousness shines upon us, if we retreat into the dungeon of despair, we will not perceive His presence, even though He shines most brightly.

Failing to Recognize the Work of Christ

We often fail to recognize when Christ is within us because we base our judgment on sensations and expect extraordinary feelings of joy, leading us to rely on *false* indicators. Every sinner imagines that Christ's arrival will bring about remarkable changes, sometimes setting unrealistic expectations for His presence.

Gideon, in Judges 6:13, made the mistake of judging God's presence on incorrect assumptions. He was unaware that God was with him not only to alleviate his suffering but also to assist him through it. This is similar to a humble sinner overwhelmed by the awareness of their sins; when told by ministers that "The Lord is with you, you broken sinners," they question why they are facing such trials if God is *indeed* with them. They compare their experiences to the miracles and victories over sin seen in the lives of saints like David, Elijah, and Paul, and wonder why *they* still struggle with their sins. The truth is, God's presence aids in the fight against sin as much as it does in overcoming it. The Apostle Paul, who once triumphed over his sins, also experienced being led captive by them, illustrating that even the presence of Christ does not guarantee freedom from struggle. "But I see another law in my members, warring against the law of my mind, and bringing me into captivity to the law of sin which is in my members," (Rom. 7:23).

The misconception lies in believing that if Christ is present, no challenges or "traitors" will remain within us. This is a flawed understanding; a heart burdened by sin may expect to be elevated to a position of honor by Christ's arrival. This expectation of feeling a specific way or achieving a certain level of spiritual experience as evidence of Christ's presence is a grave error. We are reluctant to believe Christ is with us unless we *feel* embraced by His love, judging by our *feelings* rather than by *the promises of God*.

Like Jacob, who doubted his sons' words about Joseph's survival until he saw the chariots sent by Joseph, we too doubt Christ's presence until we see clear evidence that aligns with our expectations. Despite God's word assuring us of Christ's presence, unless we feel overwhelmingly victorious over sin, we remain unconvinced of His presence within us.

Our inability to recognize Christ can also stem from being preoccupied with our own troubles, whether it be the sting of conscience, the pressure of temptation, or worldly concerns. When our minds are consumed by these distractions, we cannot perceive Christ, even if He is near. This is similar to the disciples on the road to Emmaus who, despite feeling their hearts burn within them as Jesus spoke, failed to recognize Him due to their preoccupation with their own thoughts and disappointments. "But their eyes were holden that they should not know him," (Luke 24:16).

Lastly, Christ may choose to hide Himself as a consequence of our actions. When believers fall into serious sin or make peace with their inner corruptions, God may withdraw His felt presence as a form of discipline. Obedience is a condition for God's presence, and if we stray, it is understandable for Christ to pull back, prompting us to renew our commitment and seek Him afresh. Additionally, when we take God's grace for granted and become negligent, He may distance Himself to teach us the value of His favor and encourage a more earnest pursuit of His presence.

The Lord sometimes conceals Himself as a preventive measure, choosing not to allow some of His followers to fully perceive His favor. This is to prevent them from becoming arrogant about their privileged status and looking down on their fellow believers. He offers just enough mercy to provide some comfort while keeping them humble. If a parent observes their child becoming proud, they might enforce dependence to ensure better obedience. Similarly, God recognizes our hearts' tendency to rebel and keeps us reliant on Him to secure our obedience, as mentioned in John 16:12, "I have yet many things to say unto you, but ye cannot bear them now." Just as a small boat with too large sails risks being capsized rather than aided by them, so people must adjust their "sails" to fit their "boat." This analogy illustrates why God may withdraw the sense of His favor: the "sea" represents the world, and the soul, like a boat, navigates it. A modest breeze helps the journey, but too strong a wind could cause disaster. The issue lies not with the "sails" of grace but with the "boat" of the soul that cannot withstand it.

This is why many spend their lives in sorrow, only to find great assurance at life's end. A wise man once said that God does not always serve His servants a "cup of sack," meaning He does not constantly comfort them. God's comforts, superior to wine, could lead a proud heart to disdain others. Therefore, God reserves this "cup" until the end. If we become discontent with God's timing, questioning why our prayers seem unanswered or our worship unacknowledged, and if this discontentment would lead us to turn away from God and were we to receive everything we desired, then it's evident why such restraint is necessary. As expressed in Jeremiah 2:31, this dissatisfaction could lead us to declare we will no longer turn to God. "O generation, see ye the word of the LORD. Have I been a wilderness unto Israel? a land of darkness? wherefore say my people, We are lords; we will come no more unto thee?" (Jer. 2:31). In this way, it is beneficial for God to act in this manner, as we are not capable of handling *more* without risking our humility and obedience. If we could bear it, God would undoubtedly grant it.

Uses of Implantation

[Use] Given this truth, let each person take their share: to all of you who are stubborn and disobedient, unwilling to receive the Gospel of God, to all whose hearts are unbroken and spirits not humbled, I have nothing to say at this moment. But to those of you who have experienced the work of the Spirit and grace in your souls, to those who are now willingly content and resolutely persuaded to welcome Christ and open your hearts to a Savior: if there is anyone feeling hidden as described earlier, you humble, broken-hearted sinners, go on your way with comfort, knowing that the God of heaven is with you. He will not only meet you at home but also on the way; regardless of your sins, miseries, or needs, there is consolation—yes, abundant consolation—to support your heart. If you are a poor, broken-hearted sinner, *that is sufficient*. The Lord Christ will further enter your souls, and regardless of what may come, the Lord Jesus will come, and that suddenly.

But you might say, "My sins weigh heavily on me, my corruptions are like clouds overwhelming me, all my oaths and drunkenness, pride, looseness, vanity, and worldliness, all my sins assail me, their guilt remains unpardoned." If your souls are so troubled, consider what I say: are you humbled, O polluted heart? Are you burdened by your corruptions? Does your soul lament that sin is its greatest burden and wound? If only your heart could be freed from sin, your soul would find peace. If the Lord works in you humility and sees you are humbled, He will not leave you corrupted; He will come suddenly. Let all your sins accuse you, rise against you; yet, if your heart is broken for these sins and humbled by them, and you are resolved to forsake them, the Lord will come suddenly, bringing mercy to pardon and subdue all the cursed disorders that afflict you.

But you may wonder, "Will the Lord come into my soul, this wretched place, these 'mud-walls,' this abominable heart? After committing such hideous sins, will the Lord come into such a rotten cottage, such a base cursed heart as mine?" Yes, pay attention to what the Scripture says, "I stand at the door and knock; If any man will open, I will come in." He knocks at the door of every proud person, adulterer, and drunkard. If any such person will open, the Lord will come and sanctify them. If any impure wretch will sup with him, the Lord will come and cleanse them from all abominations. What comfort is this? Let Satan accuse us, and sin condemn us; if the Lord comforts us, who can dishearten us? If the Lord saves us, who can condemn us?

This comfort extends beyond sin to all forms of suffering and distress. If you are humbled, let miseries, troubles, and temptations come; Christ will always come into a humble soul. In all weaknesses, Christ will come to strengthen; in all disgraces, He will come to honor you. Even if men's favor fades as you draw closer to God, becoming estranged from those closest to you, know that your needs, whatever they may be, will not drive the Lord away. Though friends may distance themselves, the Lord will draw near to you.

Be comforted, for as the wise man says, people often exchange honor for gain; money can seem to address all worldly needs. In this way, the rich man finds comfort in his wealth, believing it can solve any problem. You, broken-hearted sinners, can go home cheerfully, eat your bread with joy, knowing the Lord accepts you. Though others may overlook you, the Lord will comfort you more and more. Know that Christ comes suddenly and provides for *all* needs. Christ assures His disciples, "Fear not, little flock, for it is your Father's good pleasure to give you the kingdom," (Luke 12:32). You may face troubles, disgrace, or persecution, but you are promised a kingdom that will bring peace, honor, and comfort.

Wherever you are, even if you feel isolated or banished, Christ will search for you, bring you back, and comfort you both now and in the future. If this does not comfort us, *it is a great pity*. Therefore, let every sorrowful soul take their share: if you have Christ, you have everything, even if you never experience another good day.

We also must make mention of the second point I want you to notice. When the Lord Jesus comes to a humbled soul, He claims it *as His own*. This happens when the soul is completely surrendered to God, allowing His mercy to work freely. At this point, the Lord takes possession as seen in Ezekiel 16:8. "Now when I passed by thee, and looked upon thee, behold, thy time was the time of love; and I spread my skirt over thee, and covered thy nakedness: yea, I sware unto thee, and entered into a covenant with thee, saith the Lord GOD, and thou becamest mine."

Question: What does this sovereign possession entail?

Answer: It is evident in two main aspects:

1. The Lord Jesus commits to protect the soul. He pledges to shield it from all harm it couldn't otherwise escape. The sinner, recognizing the depth of his sinfulness and desiring freedom yet unable to achieve it on his own, appeals to Christ. Christ then steps in, promising to settle all debts. Just as a person threatened by a powerful enemy might seek refuge under a sovereign prince's protection, so does a soul overwhelmed by sin and despair *turn to Christ*, the ultimate protector. Christ then liberates the soul from evil, akin to how cities of refuge were open to manslayers seeking asylum from vengeance, as per Numbers 35. The sinner, pursued by guilt and fear, finds sanctuary in Christ, who delivers him from the avenger's grasp. Christ takes on three significant dangers on behalf of the humble heart: the unsatisfied justice of the Father, the unconquered temptation of Satan, and the yet-to-be-subdued sin. Christ reassures the troubled soul, promising to satisfy divine justice, thwart Satan's malice, and eliminate the power of corruption.

2. The sinner perceives a just God demanding glory. When justice looms large, Christ intervenes to bail out the soul. If a person is arrested but a prominent figure vouches for him, he is set free. Similarly, when God's wrath threatens, Christ guarantees satisfaction,

providing comfort and assurance that His word is sufficient for our peace.

In this, temptation and sin are overpowered; Christ's supreme authority ensures sin and Satan's defeat. Revelation 1:18 highlights Christ's authority, symbolized by keys, to admit or exclude at will. Christ triumphs over sin and death, showcasing His victory and dominion. "I am he that liveth, and was dead; and, behold, I am alive for evermore, Amen; and have the keys of hell and of death," (Rev. 1:18).

Sin's claim to the soul is nullified; even if sin argues long-standing dominion, Christ declares it an illegitimate usurpation. Romans 8:3 illustrates Christ's judicial victory over sin, emphasizing that those redeemed by Him are freed from sin's claim. Christ's sacrifice nullifies Adam's sin, leading to liberation from sin's tyranny. "For what the law could not do, in that it was weak through the flesh, God sending his own Son in the likeness of sinful flesh, and for sin, condemned sin in the flesh," (Rom. 8:3).

The soul, in this way claimed by Christ, benefits maximally. Under Satan's rule, the soul was barren or choked by sin. Once Christ assumes control, the soul becomes receptive to grace and mercy, prepared to welcome divine gifts. This readiness to receive God's work is termed "passive receiving," making the soul a hospitable place for mercy.

The soul responds actively to God's call, echoing His voice like an echo responds to sound. This interaction, powered by the Holy Spirit, manifests as faith. The dialogue between God and the soul reflects a mutual recognition and acceptance, as seen in Jeremiah 3:22, where the soul eagerly responds to God's invitation. "Return, ye backsliding children, and I will heal your backslidings. Behold, we come unto thee; for thou art the LORD our God," (Jer. 3:22).

In understanding this, the work of Christ is unveiled as to the initial process of divine calling, as our selected text aims to explain this significant spiritual work. Now that we have Christ in our soul, we turn to the continued action of putting on Christ daily.

FINIS

Part 2:
The Soul's Possession of Christ[2]

Romans 13:14, "Put ye on the Lord Jesus Christ, and take no thought, or make no provision for the flesh to fulfill the lusts of it."

The intention of these words is to suggest to the Romans a means of living out their salvation by which they might be encouraged to perform those duties that were required at their hands. From the eleventh verse to the end of the chapter, the apostle revisits what he has told them before, that they ought to put off the old man and no longer live recklessly and with lack of restraint to fulfill their fleshly desires, but rather should *put on* the armor of God and walk as children of the light.

Because these believers found it difficult to perform the duties required of them, in response the apostle in this verse suggests: 1) put on Christ, and 2) do not provide a place for pride, lust, or malice. And in doing so, you shall be strengthened to perform whatever duty the Lord requires of you and to overcome any corruption.

---

[2] *The Soul's Possession of Christ*: Showing How A Christian Should Put On Christ, and Be Able To Do All Things Through His Strength. Whereunto is annexed a sermon preached at the funeral of that worthy Divine Mr. Wilmott, late Minister of Clare, in Suffolk. By Thomas Hooker (1586-1647) (LONDON, Printed by M. F. for Francis Eglesfield, at the sign of the Marigold in Paul's Churchyard,) 1638. *Imprimatur*. THO: WYKES. November 11, 1637.

Now if any man asks what is meant by *putting on the Lord Jesus Christ*, I answer that this principle is to be understood in a double sense.

1. We first put on Christ by faith for justification at the point when we believe in Christ, when our debts are laid to his account and his merits are applied to us. But this is not what is meant here in Romans. Reason being, this had been spoken of long before this passage. So, it is presumed that this group of Romans to whom Paul wrote had believed in Christ *already*.

2. To put on Christ is also spoken of in regard to *sanctification*, as when we find many weaknesses and much lack of grace in ourselves, and therefore being unfit for duties. Then we are to put on Christ in order to overcome our corruptions and to quicken our hearts for the performance of those services God requires of us.

This is made clear here, for once Paul instructed them to lay aside all sin as pride, malice, riotous living, and all the works of the old man, he exhorts them to put on the Lord Jesus Christ, that they may better overcome these sins and corruptions and be enlivened to every needful duty.

From this, I observe this DOCTRINE: they that have received Christ, that have good proof from God's word that the night is past and the day has dawned in their hearts, even these have daily need to glean comfort from Christ and grace for the performance of every spiritual service which God requires of them.

Our Savior Christ must be "put on" as a garment, and that in two respects. As when a man puts on a garment, 1) he must have it fitted for him, and 2) he must put it on and apply it to his body. The Lord Jesus Christ measures all the infirmities of his children, and then he applies suitable grace according to every man's several necessities, as in Psalm 21:5, "Glory and honor thou hast fitted for him."

And Christ not only takes account of our infirmities, he also gives suitable grace according to our conditions and situations. For example, in times of injury, he gives patience, in times of persecution, he gives courage to stand for his truth and wisdom and to respond in a godly manner. Indeed, he measures out mercy and seasonable help for every estate. The Lord gives not only a fit grace to his children, but he also provides sufficient aid and strength to apply that grace, as a man not only makes his garment fit, but he puts it on close to his body. Then he is ready for any mission or directive.

Likewise, when grace is applied, a Christian is fit to walk with God in a holy course. The Lord gives a supply of seasonable grace according to our necessities. In Luke 24:49, Christ told his disciples, ""And, behold, I send the promise of my Father upon you: but tarry ye in the city of Jerusalem, until ye be endued with power from on high." And in Acts 2:3-4 we note that God gave them an abundance of grace to fit them for their works; for they spoke as the Spirit gave them utterance. The apostles needed much wisdom and courage, and God gave them an abundance of spiritual assistance. "And there appeared unto them cloven tongues like as of fire, and it sat upon each of them. And they were all filled with the Holy Ghost, and began to speak with other tongues, as the Spirit gave them utterance," (Act. 2:3-4).

The issue of the point is this, those that are in the Lord Jesus Christ have need *every day* to receive grace and quickening power from him to enable them to discharge such duties as the Lord requires of them.

1. God is the Author of all grace; we do not possess it in and of ourselves.

2. None of us can maintain what grace we do have any further than God will enable us.

3. Neither can any man exhibit grace further than God will stand by him.

So, if grace is God's gift (Eph. 2:8-10), and if none can maintain or sustain grace even when he has it any further than God enables him, nor exercise or put forth and use his grace aright without divine assistance, then it is essential that we depend on God for what we have or do. And if grace and assistance to perform any duty comes only from the Lord Jesus, then it is very necessary that we resort and return to him daily for the same. "I am the vine, ye are the branches: He that abideth in me, and I in him, the same bringeth forth much fruit: for without me ye can do nothing," (John 15:5).

The Humility Needed

The use and implementation of this doctrinal practice shows us how humble we ought to be in our own eyes and with what fear and dread we should walk before God. If it is true that we can do *nothing* without Christ, then we must of *necessity* walk in fear and awe before him, lest he take away his Spirit from us and withdraw the comfort of his grace from our soul. The apostle exhorts us in Philippians 2:12-13, "work out your own salvation with fear and trembling. For it is God which worketh in you both to will and to do of his good pleasure."

How ought we daily to fear, lest he that now offers mercy may never offer it again, and lest he that now persuades the heart will never persuade the heart more. If all depends upon the Lord, and we have no grace except what he gives, and if we cannot maintain our grace nor have any use of it except he enables us; then let us be willing to bow before him in all obedience and submission.

As it is so that we daily need strength and quickening from Christ, then look toward heaven on all occasions, and resort to the Lord Jesus for having and continuing whatever grace may be profitable and comfortable for you. I would not have a Christian only lay hold upon Christ to be justified by him. Rather, indeed, you must have your quickening grace from Christ for the performance of every action. This is the excellency of a Christian to be *all in all* in Christ, here in grace as he will be hereafter in glory.

This is the reason many Christians lay open their nakedness, and why they have so many weaknesses, because they have no recourse to Christ for grace. As it is with a scanty garment, a great part of the body is naked because the garment is not sufficient to cover it all. So is grace that is in ourselves alone. We have little patience, little wisdom, and little humility. In this way, the name of God is dishonored by us because we do not resort *to Christ* to increase our spiritual growth and to receive new strength and ability from him to help us in all duties. If we would go to Christ to have our garments sufficient for our needs, how graciously and sweetly might we walk instead?

Now it may be that some poor soul will be ready to say, "Oh, it is true. I confess there is grace and power enough in the Lord Jesus, and I have daily need to go to Christ for succor and strength. But how may I get this grace from Christ?"

For an answer, consider two things: First, in what regard we must put on Christ. And secondly, by what means we may put on Christ and draw virtue from him. If we can appropriate these two aspects of *putting on Christ*, we may walk with sufficient grace forever after.

Putting on Christ in Three Ways

Now we must put on Christ in three respects, or three ways.

1. We must "put on Christ" as Savior, that our sins may be pardoned and that joy and peace may continue for us, for there is no pardon for sin, no assurance of God's love, no peace of conscience, no joy in the Holy Spirit but only from Christ. In Luke 1:47 Elizabeth said, "My soul rejoices in God my Savior." So though we may be guilty of breaching God's commandments and liable to all his judgments threatened for the same, let us put on the Lord Jesus Christ to save us. And when we are at odds with God, by reason of our sins, let us put on Christ as a peacemaker between him and us.

2. We must "put on Christ" as Lord to cover all our sins and corruptions for us; for he comes not only to save us from sin, but to give us power to overcome all our sins. As David said, "Uphold me with thy free Spirit," or as the word is in the original, "Lord establish me with thy kingly spirit." He calls it free because kings give great gifts freely. It is as if he had said, "My heart is very weak and my affections out of order, Lord give me your kingly spirit. And though I cannot command my heart, Lord you command it; and though I cannot conquer these mighty lusts of mine, Lord, conquer them for me."

Paul said, "Thanks be to God who has given us victory through our Lord Jesus Christ, for we are more than conquerors through him that loved us," (1 Cor. 15:57; Rom. 8:37). Only here is the difference of how men conquer, and how we conquer through Christ. When men conquer, they suffer loss and they are unsure of victory. We conquer without loss, and we are ensured of victory *through Christ*. "Forasmuch then as the children are partakers of flesh and blood, he also himself likewise took part of the same; that through death he might destroy him that had the power of death, that is, the devil," (Heb. 2:14). The Lord Jesus conquered all our enemies by his death, satisfying the justice of God, and domineering over the power and malice of sin and hell for us. Therefore, put on Christ, that by virtue of his death and resurrection Satan may be subdued in your life.

    3. We must "put on Christ" as an anointed priest that we may be fitted for every duty which God requires of us. We are made priests to God the Father, through Christ, "Ye also, as lively stones, are built up a spiritual house, a holy priesthood, to offer up spiritual sacrifices, acceptable to God by Jesus Christ," (1 Peter 2:5). See how Christ triumphed over sin and hell by the power of his resurrection and holds the keys of hell and death. Therefore, let us put on the power of his resurrection that our souls are empowered to rise from the grave of sin and to walk forever in newness of life.

    Some will say, "We know there is comfort in the Lord Christ, and that he can conquer all our sins for us, and that we ought to put him on daily. But how may we do this?"

Three Means to Put on Christ

There are three means especially by which we must put on Christ.

1. We must put off something before we can put something else on. Now there are two things to be put off. First, put off all your beloved abominations and all those sins and lusts and corruption. Though temptation comes from within and occasions for temptations arise around us, do not be overcome by any sin. For by these means you withdraw yourselves from the assistance of the Lord Jesus, and his Spirit cannot take any place in your hearts. His grace cannot work because *you* allow sin to work in you instead.

Therefore, let us put off all our deceptions, lusts, and corruptions, and when we have shed them, we shall be fit to receive grace. The angel spoke to Joshua, "Put off your filthy garments, and I will give you change of raiment." Abundance of grace carries you on in a good course. If we live in the spirit, let us walk in the spirit. And how do we do that? "Let us not be desirous of vain glory, provoking one another, and envying one another," (Gal. 5:26). If we allow pride and vain glory, you cannot walk in the spirit. Christ Jesus must be Lord in your heart; Christ must be nearest the soul.

The second thing that must be put off is this, we must *renounce ourselves*. We must renounce all sufficiency and ability that is in us, that we may be under the power and assistance of the Spirit. He that trusts himself and his own ability can never receive any supply of Christ's grace to strengthen him. In this way, the apostle notes, "Oh that I might be found in him not having mine own righteousness," (Phil. 3:9).

Before his conversion, Paul boasted in the fact that he was a Pharisee. But when the Lord Christ saved him, he rent his pharisaical robes into pieces. For he counted his former garments as nothing; he cast it all at Jesus' feet.

As it is with a boat that sits partly in the stream and partly on the ground, so long as it is this way the stream cannot carry it. But move the boat fully into the stream, and then it glides along easily. So it is with our souls, if we try depending partly upon Christ and partly upon our own strength, the power of our Lord Jesus Christ will never carry us nor enable us to cheerfully go forward in a Christian course. It is true, the Lord has given us power to do what he requires. But the first activity of grace is not in ourselves. The fountain is Christ, and to him we must go first, and from him we have our graces supplied and strengthened.

The reason many Christians find themselves weak and their corruptions strong is because they look only to themselves. And when temptation stirs, such a one will begin to argue with his own heart saying, "never has any man had such a wicked heart as I have." And by this he is even more troubled than before. Instead, he should go to Christ for grace. Sin in our souls is too hard and strong for our own power to fight, but it is not too hard for the grace that is in Christ, the fountain of holiness. Like a child who cannot walk aright unless his father leads him, if we look to ourselves we end up in the wrong place. We are all such children in that though we have some grace, Christ must yet quicken us by his Spirit, raising us up and supporting us by his grace. Then we can walk cheerfully.

The reason a poor weak Christian walks comfortably while an older saint often stumbles is because when an old Christian gains a little wisdom and grace, he thinks he can go forward alone. But he then loses peace, and many times the Lord withdraws his Spirit, which leads him to fall into sin that gets the upper hand of him. Whereas a poor soul that sees his own weakness seeks Christ earnestly to raise up his heart and strengthen him with his grace, and this man walks cheerfully. While little children are under the care of the nurse, they are safe. But when they are no longer under the care of the nurse, they are at greater risk for falling, sometimes into the fire and sometimes into the water. So it is with us, while we go with the hand of Christ, looking for grace from him, we receive much strength and succor from above. But when we begin to trust ourselves saying, "What need do we have to look up to Christ now? God has enlightened us, and pardoned our sins, and given us grace. Now we can do this ourselves," it is then that we fall most shamefully, losing all our peace and assistance from Christ.

Suppose a child and old man are swimming. The child that knows how to swim commits himself to the stream, and so he swims easily. But the strong man who thinks he can do it of himself will not allow the water to carry him, so he stands with one foot on the ground and strikes the water with the other until finally he sinks and is drowned. So it is with a poor soul, when he commits himself to the stream of God's grace, he goes on comfortably in a Christian course. But when we rest upon our own ability, on what we can do, the Spirit of grace does not carry us, nor do the promises of God assist us. How can we subsist, for it is not in man to direct his own ways? Paul said, "I live, and yet not I, but Christ who lives in me," (Gal. 2:20). That is, I must first be (as) dead in myself before I can live in Christ. So should every child of God say, "I do not have life in and of myself; it must be given me from above."

The Second Means of Putting on Christ

The second means by which Christ may be put on is this, when the soul is once made naked, faith then takes the glorious robe of God's grace and brings it home to the heart. For faith is not only a hand that lays hold onto Christ for justification; it is also a shield that receives virtue from Christ for our further sanctification. Christ is the fountain of all grace, and faith is the conduit which conveys grace from Christ to the soul.

Faith in Motion

Now faith helps us in these three particular actions.

First, it is faith that closes with the Spirit of grace. In every promise of God, his Spirit of grace accompanies the same. Our Savior said, "The words that I speak to you are Spirit and they are life," (John 6:63). So, when the soul of a Christian can close with the promise, it closes also with the *grace* in the promise. For they that are in Christ are one Spirit with him. "If the Spirit of Christ be in you, the body is dead, because of sin, but the Spirit is alive because of righteousness," (Rom. 8:10). We have the most great and precious promises given to us, that by them we should be partakers of the divine nature; for laying hold of the promises, we close with the Spirit and thereby are partakers of the divine nature. I compare the Spirit of grace to the seal, and the soul to the wax, and faith is the hand which affixes the seal. By faith we cause the Spirit to work and fit its particular role for leaving an impression of grace upon the soul.

And faith not only closes with God's Spirit in the promise, it also looks at that particular grace in Christ which we stand in need of that it may be brought to bear upon our hearts. For example, if a man lacks patience, love, wisdom, humility, or the like, faith closes with the promise and brings the promise into the soul as if it were stamped upon the soul, as John 1:16 indicates, "Of his fullness have we all received grace for grace." That is, whatever grace is in Christ, we receive the same from him. As he was patient, he makes us so; as he was wise, and meek, and holy, he makes us so. Faith looks at all the particular graces that are in Christ. And as the same power that is in the head is also in the ear, and eye, and hand, so the same Holy Spirit which wrought grace in the humanity of Christ works patience in adversity and courage to bear persecution; it enlightens a man's eyes and turns his gaze toward heaven.

As the apostle reminds us, "We all behold as in a mirror the glory of the Lord with open face and are changed into the same image; from glory to glory, as by the Spirit of the Lord," (2 Cor. 3:18). The glory of the Lord is nothing but the glorious grace of God; and beholding it is when we see the glorious grace given to Christ. And again, the same Spirit that made Christ meek and wise and holy is the same Spirit that makes us poor in spirit and meek-hearted, like him. Therefore, do not look to Christ for grace in general, but for particular strength and assistance in every performance.

3. The last act of faith not only closes with the promise looking at that particular grace which is in Christ, but faith draws virtue from the Lord Jesus so that his grace may be conveyed into the soul. Therefore, the prophet says, "with joy shall you draw water from the wells of salvation," (Isa. 12:3). When a sinner with full persuasion settles himself with what God has promised, it shall be done to the soul. "A new heart will I give you

and I will put my Spirit into your hearts and cause you to walk in my ways." He not only gives grace but quickens that grace and causes men to walk holily and sweetly.

Further, if faith finds the heart dejected, unfit to pray, see how it grips and lays hold on the promises saying, "Lord, you said you would cause your people to walk boldly in your way, oh give me courage and strength." As that poor woman by touching the hem of Christ's garment drew virtue from him, so faith lays hold of the hem of Christ's garment and thereby gains refreshment.

3. The third and last means to put on Christ is that of meditation, when the soul turns itself wholly to that grace which is in Christ. Having denied ourselves, our own lusts and pseudo-sufficiencies, and having closed with the promise and the Spirit of grace in the same, this meditation keeps the soul connected to the stream of living water. As the branch cannot bring forth fruit except it abide in the Vine, no more can we, except we abide in him. We abide in Christ when the eye is fixed upon Christ, when the tongue continually speaks of Christ, when the mind dwells on him, and when the affections are directed towards him. But when the mind is taken off the promise and the comforts found therein, amusing itself by thinking of temptations or inward corruptions, then we are overcome.

If the devil can get your minds *off* the promises and on your corruptions, he has succeeded. There is a fountain of grace in Christ and in the promise, and there is a fountain of corruption in ourselves. Meditating on who we are and what we have, what we do and what we deserve leads only to fear, horror, and discouragement, the fountain of corruption.

Meditation a Grand Help

The nature of meditation is excellent for training the mind to dwell on God's promises, evidenced in these three particulars.

First, when we bring Christ and his grace nearer to us, it places the promise within our reach. As David said, "Thou through thy commandments hast made me wiser than mine enemies, for they are ever with me; and I have more understanding than all my teachers, for thy testimonies are my meditation," (Psa. 119:98-99). Meditation keeps God's commandments and statutes within reach. It brings Christ near and his promises close to the soul. If pride attempts to creep in, then meditation brings the humility of Christ to the forefront. If covetousness shows up, meditation preempts it with the heavenly mindedness of Christ. And so it is with all other sins. You people of God, whatever condition you find yourself in, if you hold fast to a constant meditation of the promises of God, you will see that grace come from heaven into your souls.

Secondly, meditation gathers up all the power that is in the promise and restores and recharges the soul with the same. As Hebrews 13:5 states, "I will never leave you nor forsake you." Meditation says, "There is infinite mercy and wisdom, compassion and goodness in my God, who will never leave me nor forsake me." It is enough, it is a free, gracious, constant and faithful promise, and I may safely rest upon it. In this way, the soul is fully contented and quieted, though all other comforts in the world fail.

We can be taken with so little, discouraged with every little trouble, because we don't consider the excellency of the promise. And yet the promise is *mine*. I thank God it is mine, and I would not be without it for anything. It is far sweeter than all the riches, pleasures, and profits of the world. Oh brethren, why should these difficulties delude us? And why are we so dismayed at the loss of these things here below? It is because we do not appreciate the excellency of the promise and the treasures from above. Christ is rich, and he is mine. If I am a wretched creature in myself, I know still that Christ is blessed and beloved of his Father. The earth is the Lord's, and the fullness thereof. And he will deny me *nothing* that is good. In conclusion, if God be mine, then all is mine.

As with a garment, the fuller it is, the more comely it is. So it is when meditation brings all the promises home. There is abundance of power in the Lord Jesus when meditation is employed. There is mercy enough in Christ, and all his goodness from everlasting to everlasting is mine when meditation contents itself upon the soul. "I have set God ever before my eyes, and because he is at my right hand, I cannot be moved," (Psa. 16:8). That is, God will give me sufficient aide and assistance in all my troubles.

When a man sets his mind on God, thinking of little else but Christ, how joyous may such a one be? But when the heart of a man searches for sufficiency from within, or some glory from without, this removes the power of the promise from him. If the preacher sees only the Lord and gives himself wholly to his disposal and receives all his strength from him, what does he care what men think or say of him? This is how you find an abundance of peace and comfort from the Almighty.

The third work of meditation is this, it secures the promise more strongly upon the soul, as it were, riveting the soul to the promise, so much so that God's child thinks and talks of nothing but the promise. Thus, the Lord Jesus is so near and dear to him that if any temptation or misery comes, he does not regard them. As Solomon said, "Take fast hold of instruction; let her not go. Keep her; for she is thy life," (Prov. 4:13).

"As you have received Christ, so walk you in him," (Col. 2:6). Walk in the power and Spirit of Christ and let the virtue received from him appear in your lives and conversations. Being clothed with the robe of Christ, our behavior should be holy. And when any temptation comes, we may have recourse to the Lord for succor! Such that if the soul is troubled with pride or hatred or revenge, look up to heaven and say, "Lord, it is not in me to tame my own heart. Lord, do your work of grace in me because it is not in this sinful heart of mine to be humble. It is not in my power to bear with personal insult and injury. But Lord, there is infinite power in you! O! blessed Redeemer, let that good Spirit that wrought humility in you work the same in me; give me a meek and heavenly heart."

And if the promise does not come suddenly, *look up once again*, and say, "Lord, you have said you will make your servant walk humbly before you, is this not a free, constant, and faithful promise?" Meditate on this promise and at last grace and aid will come to make you humble.

You must *put on Christ*, not only in the morning in prayer time and then leave him in your house or closet. For you have as much need of your garments abroad as in the house, therefore wear Christ all day long. Put on Christ continually, be able to converse and trade in Christ. Put on Christ in everything; in buying and in selling, in eating and in drinking, in *all* things. When you have any duty that needs to be done, consider what grace is most needful and go to him for the same. If this practice were established in us once for all, how holy and God-honoring should we live! As Paul said, "It is the Lord Jesus that lives in me;" so we should say, "It is the Lord Christ that does all things in me."

Dwelling in God

Little children, dwell in God. Do you desire grace? Go to the Lord Christ and put him on. He will take measurement of all your wants, he will enable you to do whatever is commanded. He that thus walks with Christ here, shall live with him forever hereafter. Many a man in his death knows what he has in the world and how to dispose of it all. But he does not know what shall become of himself, when he is gone from here. O! what a comfort it would be if he had ever conversed with Christ here, to know he shall enjoy everlasting communion with him in heaven. He shall go to his Savior that has been in him and has walked with him and communed with him here, and he shall have fullness of joy at his right hand forever.

No Advantage to Satan or the Flesh

The second means is this: we must not give any advantage to Satan nor our own flesh (by which is meant original corruption that takes possession of the whole man). The lusts of the flesh is that inclination the natural man has to any evil as well as that which withdraws a man from any good. These include pride, malice, worldliness, engaging the soul to commit any evil. We fulfill the lusts of the flesh when we bring these inward, evil desires of the heart into outward practice.

Scripture states, "Make no provision for the flesh to fulfill the lusts thereof," (Rom. 13:14). From the latter clause of this verse we may observe these three points:

1. The best of God's children (though they are spiritual and holy) have flesh and corruption in them.

2. This corruption stirs up many inclinations to sin, to draw us to commit evil, and hinders us from much good.

3. We must not create opportunities or make provision for our corruptions. This is made clear by the Spirit of God throughout Scripture (for example, Prov. 23, Deut. 12).

Making Provision for the Flesh

But here the question may be asked, what does it mean *to make provision* for the flesh?

This implies three particulars especially.

1. When we focus our meditation upon those sinful corruptions that stir within us, always thoughtfully poring over them, we warm our wicked hearts. The adulterer thinks of his liaisons and remembers the sweetness of those sins; the wrathful man increases his impatience by meditation, saying "how I've been wronged," and so the heart becomes inflamed again with anger.

The heart may settle its thoughts upon a man's lusts, poring over this and that misery, and of the dangerous hazard he and his may come to. But it may also fasten itself upon some sin, breeding consent, delight, and desire, until he resolves he will have it. This is one way we make provision for the flesh, *i.e.*, through meditation.

2. The second work of provision lies in consultation, as when the soul resolves to have its lusts, in order to injure another or to vent malice. It sits in counsel as it were as to how to contrive that which the soul longs after.

He consults about the time when, the place where, and the means by which his lusts may be attained, as with Ahab who desired Naboth's vineyard, and his wife Jezebel who contrived a way to get it for him (1 Kings 21) – a scheme that resulted in the death of Naboth and consequently the judgment of God upon Ahab, Jezebel, and all their house.

3. The last work of provision is putting into practice those cursed means which the heart has plotted and attained (*cf.* Proverbs 7). When we refuse to meditate upon our lusts, when we do not consult them, and provide no means to practice or fulfill the same, it cannot be said that we make provision for the flesh.

Firstly, this doctrine condemns those whose attention, care, efforts, and diligence are wholly spent fulfilling their carnal cursed heart's desires. As Solomon warns, "Enter not into the path of the wicked, and go not in the way of evil men. Avoid it, pass not by it, turn from it, and pass away. For they sleep not, except they have done mischief; and their sleep is taken away, unless they cause some to fall," (Prov. 4:14-16). In this way they make *provision* for the devil. They keep company with him, they sit at the same table, and their hands are in the same dish with him. It is their sustenance to practice whatever gives Satan and their own cursed heart pleasure. What is this but to provide for the flesh?

Secondly, those who cannot curb their tongues to speak evil and their hands to do evil are also here reproved. If a man can bridle himself in some outward evils, he may muse his lusts and give his wild heart liberty to think what he will. But his case is clear, meditation is the hold of Satan, the sinews of all corruptions. The mind is the very shop and warehouse of all wickedness, from which comes drunkenness, adultery, and every work of darkness. This type of meditation is as the anvil where all sinful actions are forged. All sinful devices are first framed inwardly, and then we bring them forth into practice outwardly.

I compare meditation to the distilling of waters, for it is a distillation of our corruptions and draws out the heart and life of them. See how a man distils covetousness and draws life and power from it. Everything that he sees is his own, and he wishes all his friends dead that he might enjoy all their goods. God notes complaints of Jerusalem in this very way, not only for the sins of their lives but of their hearts. He does not say, "How long shall your adulteries or drunkennesses remain?" but rather, "How long shall your vain thoughts lodge within you?"

Some will say, "What if a man cannot get power against them, what danger is there?" The Lord tells me what danger there is, "Oh Jerusalem, wash your heart from wickedness, wash your heart that you may be saved." It is as if he had said, "this heart and thought of wickedness will deprive you of heaven." So the Lord says to you, "wash your hearts you adulterous, and wash your hearts you drunkards, and you covetous wretches." For when a man's meditations are consumed with such sins, and he is content with it, this is clear evidence of one who never had the power of grace in his heart. As Solomon said, "A man of wicked devices he will condemn, for he has enough to sink his soul forever." He does not say, "a man that has practiced wickedness outwardly," but, "he that is a man of wicked meditations, always thinking of his lusts and corruptions." To this one the Lord says he will condemn him for it. So I beseech you brethren, for Christ's sake, take notice of it, and not only be aware of your outward sin, but also of every sinful imagination and the contemplative wickedness of your soul. Let me ask you as the Lord asked his people, "How long shall thy vain thoughts lodge within thee?" (Jer. 4:14).

Point of Instruction

Secondly, here is a point of instruction, to know how to judge those who are daily devising and consulting how to draw others from a good course. Sometimes a carnal friend, and sometimes a cursed neighbor, labors either by wicked counsel or by discouragements of some devilish devices to draw a man from a holy course and from the power of godliness. Whoever such a one is, judge him a partner with the devil and as one that makes provision for his lusts. I may fitly compare such wicked counselors to the devil's purveyors; they bring all their provision to his storehouses. These vile wretches would stuff our hearts with their cursed devices and carnal reasons, to draw God's people away *from* godliness. Do not permit these purveyors of hell to take up residence in your house or have a place in your heart.

When our Savior Christ told Peter that he must go to Jerusalem and suffer many things of the elders and high priests and be slain, Peter took him aside and began to rebuke him, saying, "Master, pity (or favor) thyself, these things shall not be unto thee." This was the counsel of Peter (or rather the devil in him). But see how Christ shakes him off, "But when he had turned about and looked on his disciples, he rebuked Peter, saying, Get thee behind me, Satan: for thou savourest not the things that be of God, but the things that be of men," (Mark 8:33).

So, when carnal friends say, "Oh, away with this praying," and, "why do you need all this strictness in sanctifying the Lord's day and the like." Beware of such, for these are demons of darkness, the devil's purveyors, who would lay up their provision in your hearts that you may give entertainment to Satan. Therefore, shake them off, as Christ did Peter, saying, "Get thee behind me Satan."

Making Provision Yields Obedience to Sin

The fourth and last point from these words is this, he that makes provision for his corruptions shall certainly be overcome by them; he that provides for sin shall certainly be drawn to yield obedience to sin. "Make no provision for the flesh," for it is understood if you do provide for them, you will fulfill the lusts of the flesh.

In conclusion, a provider for lust will be a fulfiller of lust; he that gives way to occasions of sin will be overtaken with such occasions. Surely, touching and defiling go together; so it was from the beginning, and so it will be to the end of the world.

As it was with Eve, the only way for the devil to overtake her was to negotiate with her. First, he works to make way for thought and meditation, and in doing so he does not speak anything affirmatively, but rather raises a question to fish out an occasion that he might take advantage. He asked, "Hath God said, you shall not eat of every tree in the garden?" And Eve answered him, "Of the fruit of the tree which is in the midst of the Garden, God has said, "Ye shall not eat, lest ye die." When the devil saw that she was (as it were) discontented because she was not to eat the fruit of that one tree, he was glad and said, "Ye shall not die at all, but when you eat thereof you shall be as gods." She allowed Satan's provision and so was overcome.

Another proof is found in James 1:15, "When lust has conceived, it brings forth sin, and when sin is finished, it brings forth death." It's like a fish when the fisherman throws in his bait. First the fish looks at it, then follows it, and afterward feeds upon it. So it is with the soul that begins to look toward a lust and fixes his meditations upon it. When lust has conceived, it brings forth sin. In the conception of lust, sin is generated in the heart as it is with corn that is sown in a field. If the ground is fit for bearing, first the earth warms the seed; then it conveys moisture into it. Next it springs forth a blade, and so grows up until it comes to produce the fruit of the ear of corn. So it is with the soul, the spawn of corruption is original sin, but meditation warms it and consultation provides moisture to feed it. Soon the fruit of sin is seen in practice, sin that results in damnation and death.

Our Savior said that out of the abundance of the heart the mouth speaks (Matt. 12:34). A man conceives a corruption when his own vile heart is stirred up to sin, then his mind is settled upon that thing, and in time it comes to fruition in life.

It is notable in the life and example of Samson. He is attracted to Delilah, then he associates with her, then sets his heart to have her, falls asleep in her lap, and at last loses his hair and thus his strength. No matter if a man is as strong as Samson in faith and grace, if he plays loosely with occasions to sin, he will in the end be defeated by his wicked desires.

But how is it that if a man provides for his flesh, he becomes a slave to his lusts?

There are two reasons:

First, in regard to sin itself, because in doing so we give great advantage to sin.

Secondly, in regard to grace, we greatly hinder the work of grace when we make provision for the flesh and give advantage to sin.

1. By making provision for the flesh, as I have shown, we give much advantage to sin and Satan who lies in wait to disrupt our Christian walk. In much the same way that we kindle and grow the graces that are given us (2 Timothy 1:6), corruption may be quickened and set ablaze by meditation because the sin nature is ever present in the natural man. All it needs to come to life is a little blowing on the flame.

Suppose a man before his conversion was given to drunkenness but God has drawn him away from that to himself. One might think he should never be drunk again. And yet the natural ("old") man is not wholly dead; and sadly what pains do we take daily that this old man may live within us? We keep him warm; we quicken that cursed disposition that is in us and we stir up that wickedness that lies dormant in our hearts.

By such means the old man begins to gather life again, he stands up and walks; so much so that the poor soul begins to fear, and is forced to say, Good Lord, was my heart ever thoroughly broken for these sins?

It is no wonder, brethren, for you make too much of the old man. You pour life into him by thinking how pleasing these fleshly means and sinful courses *were*. And by doing so, you provide strength and a foundation for corruption to prevail over you. As it is with fire, if a man has plenty of wood, though he starts with a little coal of fire, every man would say that by blowing, it will be a great flame in the end. So, there is still a coal of corruption in us all. There is a coal of pride, idleness, and deception. A cursed body of death remains in the best of us and will always remain there while we carry these houses of clay with us. But a man by meditation and consultation kindles this coal, they bring the wood, they blow on the fire, until they realize they are overtaken and cry out in misery. Why do you blow on the fire?

When an enemy lies in the field to besiege a city, if he has neither meat nor munition, he will not tarry long. But if the people within send him provision, it should not surprise them when they are overthrown by him. So meditation makes provision, and consultation sends it to the enemy.

Adding Strength to Corruptions

The second part of this reason is that as we add strength to our corruptions, meditation is as an invitation of the devil to come and tempt us. It is as if we give money to the devil by subjecting ourselves and our souls to the powers of temptations as occasions are offered to us, so that we must either be captivated or overtaken by them.

When we think highly of our own abilities to withstand such occasions of temptation, it is as if we are setting open the doors for the devil to come and commune with us. Whatever the heart's meditations are set upon, the heart is under the power and strength of that sin so that in time it prevails with him and domineers over him.

As it is with floodgates, when they are set open, it lets in the rush of the river that carries all that came before it. So meditation upon any occasion sets open the floodgate, that it carries the soul's predispositions to the practice of any sin.

For example, a covetous man is under the power of that lust. Give him opportunity, and he will covet and potentially steal. The devil was well aware of Judas' covetous heart, so the devil put it in the mind of Judas to betray the Lord. Even if the Master escapes, you will gain from it. In this way, Satan took possession of him and prevailed with him to do that for which he had formerly consulted about. By giving way to the devil, he was overcome by him.

If by meditation and consultation we give strength to our corruptions by yielding to the flesh, then the devil will overcome us. By this provision we give force and power to our lusts, making way for them, submitting ourselves to them, and therefore shall be overcome by them.

Hindering Grace

The second reason is taken from the hindrance of the work of grace, whereby we might be fortified against our corruptions. We do that in these two ways.

1. By daily musing of our sins and corruptions we kill the work of grace in our hearts, in so much that it is either dead and will not work, or else it is rendered inferior so that it cannot work. This meditation and consultation so consume the soul, such that the heart has no liberty to work; no room is left for faith, patience, and heavenly mindedness.

When a man lets out all his mind and thoughts, his reason, affections, and desires after his lusts, it is no wonder such a one cannot believe. What is become of faith, and hope, and patience in him? They are all making provision for the flesh. There is no room left for faith that sits alone in the soul, because the whole stream of the heart and mind is employed in hunting after vanities.

Now if while in this condition you ask the poor soul if he has any assurance of God's love or any stirrings of grace, he will answer no. The reason is because they have spent all their thoughts in fear, and doubting, and discouragement, and were all making provision for these. And in the meantime, faith lays as dead in the soul. Though faith works in the soul, it must use the soul and all the affections of it, as the memory, understanding, and desires; it cannot work without these. The soul of a man being a finite creature, cannot settle its affections upon many objects at once. If he gives his mind to sin and the occasions thereof, he cannot meditate upon Christ and the promise. When a man allows the stream of his desire, judgment and endeavor wholly for the flesh and the world, there is nothing left for Christ, and grace, and the cause of God.

David was a wise man, and yet when Nabal had wronged him, see what provision he made for his anger, "Surely in vain have I kept this fellow and all that he had in the wilderness. So and more also do God unto the enemies of David if I leave of all that pertains to him by the morning's light..." (1 Sam. 25:22 and following). Then Abigail, Nabal's wife meets David, bearing gifts, and is able to pacify his anger against Nabal, in so much that David said to her, "Blessed be God, and blessed be thou, and blessed be thy counsel to me."

Why was Abigail able to counsel David when he was unable to counsel himself?

Though David was a righteous man, and wise, he had so given over his heart to wrath that he had no room for any work of wisdom or patience to take place, and in that instance stood in need of a counselor himself.

In such cases we deprive ourselves of the comfort and virtue of the promise that otherwise we might enjoy. The Spirit and promise of God is that which helps a Christian in all his problems. However, the work of the

Spirit of grace *dies in the heart by meditation of sin;* forgetting God's promise stops the stream of his goodness so that we do not receive that grace that we might otherwise be strengthened by. God communicates grace to us from his promise, but we must look for it, and turn our mind and thoughts toward it. But when a man turns his meditations upon the world and the occasions thereof, he has turned completely aside from the promise. And not meditating upon the promise and its means of grace, he can receive no strength nor comfort from the same.

Hebrews 12:3 says, "Consider him that endured such contradictions of sinners against himself, lest ye be wearied and faint in your minds." Here are two observations from this passage:

First, the Lord Jesus Christ is able to make us strong and resolute in mind that we shall not faint at the opposition of sinners.

Secondly, we must consider him, which is to say we must set our hearts and our affections upon him. As if he had said, "You are unable to be patient and to endure injuries, but consider him that did, and then you shall receive strength and power to suffer patiently."
Now I come to the Uses, which are of great weight. Therefore, read them carefully.

One such use that is both powerful and excellent is the ability to experience reform in those things that are amiss, to guide us in the way to happiness. And yet whoever makes provision for the flesh shall certainly be overcome by it. This is a ground of direction whereby a man may perceive what his own and the practices of other men are, and what will become of himself and others. Judge such by what provisions others make and by what course they undertake. If a man uses means that tend to his lusts, there's a heavy suspicion that he will be overtaken by his lusts. If a man provides for the world, the world will overtake him; and if he provides for his pleasures, they will certainly ensnare him.

If we see what provisions are in a man's house, we may easily conjecture of what sort his guests will be. As it is in housekeeping, just so it is in heart-keeping. When we see what provision a man makes for his lusts, we may know what his course will be. As the apostle said, when men do not like to retain God in their knowledge, God gives them over to a reprobate mind, to do those things which are good in their own eyes. O! wretched man, why do you spite the Spirit? If you have no Spirit, then you are a damned man. And if you do not want to acknowledge God, will he not ere long give you over to a reprobate sense.

It is a sign that a man is devoted to destruction, and even sealed to condemnation, who undervalues the knowledge and ways of God, who has no delight in Jesus Christ, and who despises the Spirit and the means of grace. And so it is in Hebrews 10:28, "he that despised Moses' law died without mercy, of how much sorer punishment is he worthy, which treads underfoot the Son of God?"

There are two things to be noted in this verse:

1. He that knows God's Law, and breaks the same willfully, dies without mercy.

2. What will become of him who opposes the mercy of Christ, tramples his blood under his feet, and makes a mockery of sanctification? I tell you, you shall receive judgment without mercy.

If you have any such condition in your heart, then you may conclude what your course will be. If you despise the Lord and his Spirit of grace, then you shall surely perish. If you see a man unable to endure the power of the Gospel in the plainness and efficacy of it, but still he is snarling against the truth and railing at the man who delivers it, know that such a one makes provision for persecution, for he has a malicious and envious heart and is full of venom and violence against God and his grace. And if opportunity presents itself, he will prove a fierce and devilish persecutor.

The case is clear, he that provides for sin will surely be overcome with sin. You saints of God do not wonder though you are despised and hated by evildoers. Let these dogs bark, and the lions roar, and let them hate you still. They provided for their lusts and corruptions and malice, and therefore they are overcome by them. You surely see the danger of listening to fleshly enticements, how they enthrall us in Satan's bondage and hinder the work of grace in our hearts.

Getting a Right Heart

How then might I get my heart to abhor every deed of darkness?

Firstly, labor for a teachable spirit. An honest heart gladly embraces the least indication of any evil, it hearkens to any information of what is amiss, by any person or means whatsoever. A gracious heart desires to be freed not only from the dominion of sin, but also from the presence of it, and is ready to take the least inkling from any occasion or speech of any saint of God to that purpose. When anyone tells him that such a course is sinful, such a practice is unlawful, he is very careful to attend unto and be advised of it.

If an enemy puts forth anything against him as a matter of scandal, that will make his heart shake within him, and he begins to consider whether such an action is warranted. The honest soul is never quieted until it is thoroughly informed of what is good and may be performed, and what is evil and must be abandoned. "What I do not know Lord, teach me. And I will hold my tongue," said Job. He does not quarrel with the man that counsels him, or wrangle with the man that advises him; but says, "teach me, and I will hear readily. If I have done iniquity, I will do so no more." He is willing to understand any failing and will not put off a godly reproof with scorn.

A gracious heart is *suspicious* of himself and seeks direction from God, that he may clearly perceive his miscarriages, and even avoid them. He looks up to heaven, and says, "Lord, you know the secrets of my heart, let me know them too. You know the framework of the soul of man, let me understand the frame of my own spirit as well, that I may not sin against you."

2. In the second place you must ask God for a *submissive mind* to do his will and yield quietly to the authority of the power of the truth. A gracious heart will not invent clever ways to defeat the Word of Life when it is evidently and plainly brought home to the conscience. Though one may rebuff a bit at the beginning, when it sees that it cannot answer the argument, it will be content to listen and learn.

As in the case of Peter, when he denied our Savior, the very look of Christ made him go out and weep bitterly. A gracious soul rejects no light to discover his ways, he easily submits to every good word of God.

3. Thirdly, commit to *reforming whatever is amiss*. Do what you can in particular and seek from Christ to do what you are unable to perform. It was a hard task which God commanded Abraham to do, which was to sacrifice his beloved Isaac. Yet when it appeared to be plainly God's command, though it were ever so hard; there was no resisting it. Abraham therefore rose early in the morning, and he and the child went immediately to discharge his duty. In the process, he disallowed all occasions that might hinder him – his wife was not acquainted with it, and his servants knew nothing of the matter.

So, if one claims to be the spiritual son of faithful Abraham, whatever the Lord commands, even to the killing of a beloved lust, if the Lord says it must be done, this sin must be avoided, this course must be amended, then the soul of a gracious man will rise early in the morning to accomplish the same.

4. Fourthly, a gracious heart eagerly desires to employ the cure that God prescribes for the killing of his corruptions that reformation may be made.

Take an arm or a leg that has been infected with gangrene, to which the doctor says you either must lose your leg or your life. If the patient says he'd rather lose his life than part with a limb, then one must conclude he cannot live long. If he purposed to maintain life, surely then he would part with that which takes away life.

Suppose a man has acquired an estate by thievery. When the Word of God comes to bear on his soul and tells him he must make it right or be damned, this man may be dejected in spirit, but nothing will cure the problem but restitution. This is the gangrene that must be cut off.

What if he replies that most of his gain has come to him in this fashion, such that if he should restore all that he unjustly gained, he should die a beggar. Then I would ask of him, but what will it profit a man to gain the whole world and lose his own soul? Is it not better to die in a poor estate than in a sinful estate? To depart a good man than a rich man?

Again, suppose a man is a minister or a great professor, and yet has been seen openly drunk or is known to have committed adultery. There is no cure for this man now, but he must satisfy the congregation which has been dishonored and discredited by his sin. So let him fast and pray, and weep. I cannot see how this man's conscience can be quieted, unless he makes public satisfaction, as his offense was public.

5. A sincere Christian welcomes those truths that are sufficiently powerful to prevail with his sins and subdue his corruptions. The Word of God is most pleasing to him that is most effectual this way.

In this way, a gracious heart seeks nothing so much as the death of sin, that there might be a new nature born in him. Therefore, he pleads with the Lord, "you take away the heart of stone, you subdue a stubborn spirit, and you master a malicious mind. I urge you, let it be according to your good Word."

When the truth of Christ lays a charge against a good man's heart, the soul willingly lies under the blow, and closes with the rebuke, saying "thank you, good Lord." A man troubled with a toothache, when the dentist applies his instrument, he says, "pull it out, leave nothing behind." So, when the soul is under the power of some violent lust, when the Word comes home to the conscience, the gracious soul says, "Lord, pull it out all, that I may never see that pride again, nor that covetousness; do not leave a stump remaining Lord, but free me wholly from this vile accursed condition."

An Old Testament prophetic passage from Zechariah has significance here, "And one shall say unto him, 'What are these wounds in thine hands?' Then he shall answer, 'Those with which I was wounded in the house of my friends,'" (Zech. 13:6). Here the messenger of God spoke friendly to me, and though he wounded my heart fully, this is a special means of divorcing the heart from sin, when it closes with such truths as tend to the awaking of it.

6. As the soul welcomes such powerful truths, it is restless until God is pleased to work and until *every* corruption and *every* sin is captured and overcome and that soul is restlessly looking and waiting upon God. The Irishman, being malicious and fearful, never thinks his enemy killed until he cuts off his head. So it is with a gracious heart which never thinks sin is mastered until it sees the very life and blood of his corruptions removed, until it sees the strength and power of sin subdued more or less within him.

Therefore, the Apostle cries out, "Oh wretched man that I am, who shall deliver me from this body of death?" Mark the weight of his complaint. He does not say, "who shall deliver me from this action of sin," but "who shall deliver me from this body of sin?" There is a body of pride, there is a body of covetousness, and a body of anger which cleaves to us. Now a gracious heart is not content to just be delivered from a tongue of pride, haughty speeches, and the like. It must be freed from the body of pride and self-love, from the frame and bent of this carnal spirit.

7. Lastly, as the soul welcomes the truth that it may do its work in the heart, though I have as much

pride as the devil, may it be done; though I be filled with sin, I desire to be purged from my filthiness. It may be done, Lord, let it be done, *whatever it costs me.*

But what shall we think of those who would rather part with their life than with their most cherished sin? These will not endure the least reproof to come near them; no means can prevail to tear their corruptions from their souls; to take the cup from the drunkard or the pleasure from the adulterer, or greediness of gain from the covetous man or woman.

When the prophet was found admonishing the people, "This is the good way, walk in it," notice how they respond. "We will walk in our own ways, and follow our own devices," and as they resolved, so they did. When God's faithful ministers would help these take hold of their pride, their lust, their uncleanness to rid themselves of it, they gain a tighter hold on their lusts, they cling to their pride and refuse to part with it; they nourish malice in their souls in spite of God and his ministers and all admonitions and directions whatsoever. But be forewarned, if you will live in your sins here, expect to be damned with them hereafter.

Some indeed will speak against their sins, confess they do evil, and resolve to reform. But how weak and disinterested they are in the work to do so. They continue to nourish secret haunts of heart. They may put forth some minimal effort, but they do not leave their corruptions. They cannot conceive of an everlasting separation between their sin and their souls.

Though sometimes the Word overpowers them, and conscience convicts them, yet they maintain the old connections and friendships still. As it is with servants in a family that intend to marry privately, though their master separate them so that they cannot dwell together, yet they will meet and confer one with another elsewhere to do so. So it is with those who may feel compelled to put away their beloved sins temporarily. They do not allow them to go far, for they must reconnect with them now and then.

When Pharaoh was battered by the hand of God, and one judgment after another pursued him so much that he could not bear it, he was content at last to let the children of Israel go. But still he did not allow them to go far before pursuing them yet again. So, if one must leave their sin but sees that it does not go far, and in so doing such a one *beguiles* their own soul. Such a man threatens his evils and strikes them in some measure, but works to not abandon them fully, so as never to have to *completely* part with them.

I beseech you to take notice of what God commands. If your brother or your friend which you love as your own soul shall entice you to adultery, separate yourself from him *completely*.

Brethren, dwell in meditation a while considering these things, and ask your heart whether sin is a *burden* to you. Am I content to part with my darling corruption? Am I content to yield up my whole man to God, to serve him cheerfully, singly, and constantly throughout the course of my life? If so, go home in peace, and the God of heaven go with you.

But if I leave my sins and I am consumed with what shall become of my riches and honor? All pleasure and contentment must then depart from me.

In your full-hearted pursuit of God, you shall not lose your comforts but exchange them for better. For what are riches without grace? There is a woe in all that wealth and poison in all that prosperity. The best things here are but temporary and mutable; what wise man would part with an eternal inheritance that does not fade away for a life of temporary pleasures?

What is it to enjoy the creature for a season but be deprived of the Creator forever? You lose nothing by embracing Christ but rubbish and filth that defiles and oppresses you. He that leaves father, or mother, or houses, or lands for my sake (Christ said) shall have a hundred fold here and everlasting happiness hereafter (Luke 18:29-30). Therefore, bring out every sin and iniquity, produce every lust and wickedness that lodges within you, and lay them down at Christ's feet. Be content to part with all, that you may enjoy him that is more than all. Who would not leave sin for a Savior, exchange darkness for light, or part with an empty contentment to be satisfied with the true never-fading good? If you will not have God take away your sins, the truth is that God will take away his grace and Holy Spirit from you.

Was there ever a man so foolish that he would not let a doctor treat him when he was sure to recover and cure from it? Consider this seriously, you must either reject your sin or reject your soul; either allow God to deprive you of your lusts or deprive you of heaven.

God hates wickedness, so if you allow sin to dwell in your heart, God will not dwell with you, nor you with him. If you harbor and hold onto your sins, *you must hold fast to shame and sorrow too.* For a stranger to grace is a stranger to God. Gratify your lusts, and you gratify the devil. Without holiness there can be no lasting happiness. Heaven is too pure a place for any unclean thing to have admission into. Consider what I say, and the Lord give you understanding in all things.

FINIS

Appendix: Spiritual Munition

Psalm 20:7, "Some trust in chariots, and some in horses: but we will remember the name of the Lord our God."

2 Kings 2:12, "And Elisha saw it, and he cried, My Father, my Father, the chariots of Israel, and the horsemen thereof..."

When the Lord revealed that he would take away Elijah in a whirlwind (2 Kings 2:1), we find that Elisha (who lived and trained under Elijah) did two things: 1) he followed him closely while he lived, and 2) he mourned for him at his death. The Lord sent for Elijah, and immediately he was transported to heaven in a fiery chariot. When Elisha could no longer see him, he cried out, "O my Father, my Father."

We observe two things in this verse: 1) the affection Elisha had for his Master, and 2) the commendation or description of Elijah.

Elisha's affection for Elijah was demonstrated by 1) His honorable esteem of him "Father," 2) His humble subjection to him, "My Father," and, 3) His lamentation and mourning for him, "O my Father," wherein the great grief and passion of his soul is displayed in the rending of his clothes (seen in the latter part of v. 12).

The term "father" is sometimes used for a natural father, and sometimes it signifies a period of time of long continuance (as "Fathers in Israel," for example).

The point I'm making here is that the ministers of God should be as Fathers to their people in these three areas: First, they should have a steadiness and gravity both of Spirit and life. "Let no man despise your youth," (Paul said to Timothy), "but be an example in life and doctrine."

Secondly, in regard to the power and authority committed to them by God, Paul used both kind words and a stern rod. Ministers must be good and wise Fathers, not flatterers of men.

Thirdly, in regard to the instruction they give their people, it must be in line with both their necessity and ability. They must be eyes to the blind, ears to the deaf, and feet to the lame.

This should therefore teach the Lord's watchmen to shine as burning lamps, to be examples of piety and strict obedience.

And you that are hearers should deal with the ministers of God's Word as obedient children listen to the instruction of their Father. As Paul states, "rebuke not an elder but entreat him as a father." If we see anything in the minister that is faulty, then we should mourn for it, and wisely suggest it to him. For we are not to believe and do in all things as the Minister says or does simply because he is the Minister. Rather, we are told to search the Scriptures and try men's doctrines, whether they be according to God or not. And if they are found to be consistent with God's truth, then we are to submit ourselves to them.

Further, we should have a reverend esteem of them and the places to which God has called them. We must entertain them as ambassadors, as co-workers with the Son for their salvation, to bring the creature and his Creator together. And for those who wish to point out the Minister's failings, then let us be reminded that we have this heavenly treasure in earthen vessels. For are not all of us full of failings?

Secondly, we are to submit and subject ourselves to the truths delivered. Willingly subject your soul to the word and labor to be under the power of divine truths revealed. We should be found saying as Samuel did, "Speak Lord, your servant hears," and as Paul said, "Lord what will you have me do?"

If a command follows, the soul should readily perform it; if a reproof is necessary, the soul should willingly bear it. Anything less would be pride and rebellion against God and his truth. This ought not to be found among Christians. If any man quarrels, taking up arms against the word of the Almighty, let that man know that his doom is certain. For God will certainly punish all such stubborn and stiff-necked rebels that refuse to have him rule over them.

Strive instead for a yielding submissive spirit, the kind of soul willing to be taught of God, to be disposed of by him in everything, to receive any impression which he desires to bring you. When you come to hear the Word, bring a teachable mind and say, "Good Lord, let this your servant now hear a seasonable word, quicken these dead bones. Speak to my conscience, wound my corruptions, slay these sins that are too hard for me, let no iniquity prevail over this poor servant, but let Jesus Christ be all in all to and in me. Take this heart of mine, frame it, alter it, mold and melt it. Work your own will in me, fashion me to your kingdom of grace here that I may partake of your kingdom of glory hereafter."

A good heart will bless God for new light, and say, "I never observed that pride, I never discovered that guile of spirit, I never took notice of such swarms of lusts lurking in my soul as you have shown me now. Before this, I did not care what became of Christ or his Ministers. I did not value nor honor nor regard the Name of Christ or His Gospel. But now I see the evil of my ways, and blessed be God for that good work which has been communicated to my soul by his servant."

Foundationally, Christians ought to respect God's Messengers. They should submit themselves to their Message. And they ought to be serviceable to them in all things. For they are conduits of God's grace. Children go to their father's house to be fed and clothed. So it should be with us.

This instruction should reprove two sorts of people: those that instead of doing good to a faithful Minister, work to see how they can root him out; and instead of subjecting themselves to the Word of God delivered through him, they maintain rebellion against it. But tell me Brethren, is he a dutiful son who casts his father out of the house? It is a sure sign that that soul never had grace which opposes the Ministers of grace. Rather, this is a fearful symptom of an unsound heart, and wherever it is found, it clearly evidences that God has forsaken that soul.

If any man has a stubborn heart, a rebellious soul, such that he will not subject himself to the Word of God, he cannot have any true peace; he may have pseudo-peace in the world, but he shall have gall in his conscience.

Some will say, "I like this man well enough, and I could love and respect one minister dearly, but not another."

But if both are God's Ministers of truth, how can you be such a respecter of persons? If he is a faithful Minister but you cannot find room in your heart to receive him and highly esteem him, it is a sign that you have no grace.

Finally, may the Ministers of God *esteem* and *prize* those beloved of God that love and obey His Word. May those saints who strive to be holy before the Lord be those that occupy your thoughts.

I leave this now and move to the commendation of Elijah.

The chariots of Israel, as well as horsemen, are used here to metaphorically represent the defense and protection of Israel. For in ancient times, they went to war with iron chariots. And those armies that had the most iron chariots were naturally believed to be the strongest. Therefore, the hearts of the children of Israel were daunted when they perceived that the Canaanites had iron chariots. And, of course, horses are warlike creatures of great strength.

Faithful Ministers, by their fervent prayers and supplications, stop the wrath and indignation of the Lord (both Moses with God's people and Abraham with Lot are perfect examples). Take heed, therefore, before you speak wrongfully of a praying Minister, for prayer is a great force.

Faithful Ministers reveal the sins of the people with whom they live, and labor to work them to godly repentance that they may turn to the Lord and thereby turn away judgments. O! brethren, we justly fear the sword. But let me tell you, it is not the weakness of our land, nor the power of the enemy, that can hurt us as much as our treacherous hearts at home. These swarms of unruly lusts and corruptions which we carry about and harbor in our bosoms daily do us more hurt than all the world besides. Our sins lay us open to God's judgments more than anything else. A faithful Minister endeavors to turn away sin, and so by consequence the wrath of God, from a place. This is a great deal of good that a man of God may do.

By this the hearts of men are made willing to yield obedience to the governors that are set over them. It makes them faithful to God and country, industrious in doing good and obedient to the Lord. This allows men to be blessings in the stations where God has placed them. For it is a certain truth that he that is disloyal to the King of heaven can never be loyal to the king of earth. This instills courage into the hearts of people, whereas sinful and base courses fill a man with continual fears and discouragements. The Lord is with us while we cleave to him; but if we forsake him, he will forsake us. It is wonderful to see what a good Minister can do to fight against principalities, and powers, and spiritual wickednesses in high places, not fearing the face of man. The clear knowledge of this, that the battle he fights is the Lord's, assures him that the Lord will fight for him. Any coward will fight when he is assured of victory beforehand. A good cause will make men spend their dearest blood. When a man has God to go before him, and the Word to warrant him in what he does, he goes through thick and thin. As evidence to this, we remember with what joy and cheerfulness the martyrs sacrificed their lives to the flames.

    This shows that those who are enemies to God's faithful Ministers are the greatest adversaries that the Church or State has, for they spoil the munition of the land. And consider this, if a man should take away all the munitions of England and transport them to Spain, every man would rightly say he is a traitor. So, if you determine to oppose and secretly undermine any man who is a true faithful Minister of Jesus Christ, know that you are a traitor to the King of heaven and earth, because you oppose the one God set to labor in this place to hold back the wrath of God from the land. Be humbled therefore, take notice of this shameful sin so that you do not let it once be named among you who are Christians. Having laid forth all this, let us live as Christ did, that we may enjoy the end of our hope, which is eternal life and joy. Brethren, while we live here, may every Minister of God be a spiritual Father to God's people in the place he has been sent.

And as such, may he be a chariot and horseman at the forefront of the battle, a main defender of the faith of Christ. Witness brethren, the heartbreaking sighs and earnest prayers that a Minister of God puts forth in the days of his service. If any sins are stirring, or any iniquity abounds, he labors by fasting and prayer to oppose the same. There are those, in fact, who are so taken with their love of the Lord Jesus and his blessed truths, that his service and endeavors extend well beyond normal human expectations.

You likely know such Ministers that often stand in the gap and labor fervently in prayer to avert God's wrath and remove his heavy judgments. Witness his strong cries and intercessions to the Almighty in a time of common calamity. Witness those painful employments that he takes up in season and out of season to exhort and rebuke with all longsuffering and patience. Sometimes alluring the heart with sweet promises, other times threatening judgment against obstinate sinners. Preaching every Lord's Day as well as throughout the week (as occasion is offered) for the good of his people. Witness also the many sweet comforts and heavenly consolations whereby he refreshes and supports many a fainting soul.

As a result, the loss of an able, true-hearted, faithful Minister, the help and fortress of a people and a nation, are greatly mourned. "O my Father, my Father," said good Elisha, as he looked wistfully on Elijah, eyes fixed constantly towards him, until he could see him no more.

Why then should we not sorrow over similar losses of our own? We hear ourselves say, "O my spiritual Father, who pointed me to the way of salvation." And another, "O my Father, by whom I was directed down the path of holiness." Or, "O my Father, by whom my soul was comforted, maintained, and nourished in spiritual things."

Brethren, let us call to mind all the prayers, and humiliation, and fasting, and supplications to the throne of grace our Ministers have initiated on our behalf. May the Lord give us strength and courage to follow in his steps, that we finish our course well.

To briefly conclude, when we lose such a one, we should double our efforts to fill in the gap and make up the hedge that has been breached for the loss of this chariot, this horseman, who has gone ahead to glory.

For consider that we do not know how soon death may knock at our own door. Our times are in God's hand, the One who takes us to himself when he pleases. Happily this day may be our last day, and this very season may be the last opportunity that I ever have to pray, to intercede, to exhort, encourage, rebuke a fellow brother before I myself meet God. Therefore, be encouraged to add one prayer more that God's army may be increased still.

And further, if ever you pray, pray now, if ever you fast, fast now; if ever you humble yourselves, be humbled now in dust and ashes before the Lord. For there has never been more need, never greater want. By this means the land will be strengthened, and our peace and safety continued.

Though our enemies are many and our sins great, fervent prayer enables a God who is stronger and mightier than them all. If you can say in truth as Hezekiah did, "Good Lord remember how I have walked uprightly before you," this will sustain a man's comfort and support his soul in the most difficult times. For a heart that does not pray is a dismal thing. Therefore, be encouraged to the duty: Pray, pray, pray.

FINIS.

Other Works from Puritan Publications Concerning *Coming to Christ*

Christ Inviting Sinners to Come to Him for Rest by Jeremiah Burroughs (1599-1646)
> Along with Gospel Worship, this is the best work Burroughs ever penned. It is one of the best puritan works you will ever read on coming to Christ.

The Efficiency of God's Grace in Bringing Gain-Saying Sinners to Christ by Simeon Ashe (d. 1662)
> How does God draw sinners to himself? In this rare puritan work Simeon Ashe teaches on John 6:44, and the manner in which God uses to drag gain-saying sinners to salvation.

A Christian's Directory by Christopher Love (1618-1651)
> Every Christian needs spiritual direction in the basics of the Christian life. How should a Christian always walk, whether in joy, or in mourning, whether in prosperity, or in poverty?

The Trial of a Christian's Sincere Love to Christ by William Pinke (1599–1629)
> God has you on trial for being a Christian...will you be acquitted? A sincere love to Jesus Christ is what is needed.

The Day of Grace by Nathaniel Vincent (1639-1697)
> One of the best puritan works ever written on coming to Christ "now"! Today is the day of grace!

Seeing Christ Clearly by C. Matthew McMahon
> How did Jesus view himself in the Gospels? Who is this divine Son of Man who comes down out of heaven? Do you see Christ clearly?

www.ingramcontent.com/pod-product-compliance
Lightning Source LLC
Chambersburg PA
CBHW020256090426

42735CB00009B/1105